An Introductory Clinical Guide to

DISSOCIATIVE IDENTITY DISORDER

Best Practices for Working with Multiplicity, Attachment Wounds, and Complex Trauma

Gregory L. Nooney, MSW, ACSW, LISW, LCSW

An Introductory Clinical Guide to Dissociative Identity Disorder

Published by
PESI Publishing, Inc.
3839 White Ave
Eau Claire, WI 54703

Cover and interior design by Amy Rubenzer
Editing by Jenessa Jackson, PhD

ISBN 9781683737780 (print)
ISBN 9781683737797 (ePUB)
ISBN 9781683737803 (ePDF)

Printed in the United States of America.

Praise for *An Introductory Clinical Guide to Dissociative Identity Disorder*

"Greg Nooney is a true ally to people with dissociative identities, and this book shows that he has done the most important study of all in developing his clinical DID specialty: listening to his clients and to those with lived experience. *An Introductory Clinical Guide to Dissociative Identity Disorder* is an excellent resource for therapists who are new to working with dissociative identities and for those who need guided structure to assist their clinical conceptualization. While each client or system with dissociative identities is unique and bringing concepts together into a single manual or resource is next to impossible, Greg does the closest thing possible with great competence. His 'best practices' structured infographic sets a great tone for the material that he offers in this book, and the voice that comes through shows his wisdom and experience."

—**Dr. Jamie Marich, PhD, LPCC-S, REAT,** founder and CEO of the Institute for Creative Mindfulness and author of *Dissociation Made Simple: A Stigma-Free Guide to Embracing Your Dissociative Mind and Navigating Daily Life* and *Trauma and the 12 Steps: An Inclusive Guide to Enhancing Recovery*

"In this brief, engaging, and very clearly written book, Greg Nooney shares the knowledge he has gained through years and years of working directly with people who experience themselves as multiple, separate identities—people who have developed dissociation as a survival skill in the face of circumstances that have threatened their very existence. It is not easy to write a 'how-to' book that avoids rigid recipes while still being useful in its guidance, but Nooney has done it. He keeps the people seeking help—their values, their specific circumstances, their longings, and their struggles—at the center, while offering useful advice for what to expect, what to avoid, and how to create an accepting, safe-enough, and hopeful space for healing."

—**Gene Combs,** co-director of the Evanston Family Therapy Center and co-author of *Narrative Therapy: The Social Construction of Preferred Realities*

To everyone living with a dissociative identity and all the therapists who work collaboratively with them.

TABLE OF CONTENTS

INTRODUCTION

Celebrities, athletes, and politicians who have been brave enough to reveal their struggles with mental health have done much to reduce the stigma of seeking help. As a result, the experience of anxiety and depression is becoming normalized. However, more serious conditions, such as dissociative identity disorder (DID), formerly called *multiple personality disorder* (MPD), remain mostly in the shadows. When the media does shed light on DID, it does so with dramatic effect, casting those with this diagnosis as uncannily mysterious and chillingly dangerous. These misleading and sensational representations of DID have not only increased the stigma associated with the disorder, but they fail to acknowledge the unspeakable childhood trauma that causes the self to fragment and makes life more difficult for those who suffer from extreme dissociation (Pullman-Moore, 2022).

Moreover, professionals in mental health circles have historically held the widespread misbelief that DID is exceedingly rare (Brand et al., 2016), so specific training has been reserved for those few therapists who decide to specialize in it. However, these therapists are often criticized as being too naive as to believe and honor the experiences of those with DID, or they have been blamed for causing the symptoms by making inappropriate suggestions toward sensitive clients. Some therapists who have stepped up to work with these clients are even accused of *creating* the condition by retrieving false memories and exaggerating common mood swings. Despite research suggesting that DID is more prevalent than schizophrenia and autism, and has approximately the same prevalence as bipolar disorder,* the belief that it is rare persists—as do other common myths, including the belief that it is a fad, that it is identical to borderline personality disorder, that it is mostly diagnosed in North America, that it is harmful to patients, and that it is an iatrogenic disorder rather than a trauma-based disorder (Brand et al., 2016).**

---

* The *DSM-5-TR* estimates the prevalence of the following mental disorders: DID 1.1%–1.5%; schizophrenia 0.3%–0.7%; autism spectrum disorder 1%–2% worldwide and closer to 1% in the United States; and bipolar I disorder 1.5% (APA, 2022).

** The *DSM III-R* (1987) revised its contention that MPD was rare as follows: "Recent reports suggest that this disorder is not nearly so rare as it has commonly been thought to be" (p. 271). The *DSM-5-TR* suggests a 1.5% prevalence (APA, 2022). According to ISSTD (2011), other studies suggest as much as 3% of the population has DID. The CDC does not consider a disease to be rare in the United States unless there are fewer than 200,000 cases (Khoury & Valdez, 2016; Valdez et al., 2016). The population

Although the International Society for the Study of Trauma and Dissociation (ISSTD; 2011) provides ample evidence that therapy is helpful in working with clients with DID, there is no established evidence-based therapeutic practice for doing this work. This leaves well-meaning clinicians at a loss when they realize that a client has sufficient symptoms to meet criteria for a DID diagnosis. Even therapists who are well-versed in childhood trauma and attachment wounds may feel ill-equipped to work with clients with DID, believing that such work is outside their scope of practice. Although they may attempt to refer these clients to another therapist, the reality is that the few therapists who do specialize in DID are likely unable to accept the referral due to full caseloads. This unfortunate truth means many clients with DID cannot receive the therapeutic help they need.

To address this need, I wrote my first book, *Diagnosing and Treating Dissociative Identity Disorder: A Guide for Social Workers and All Frontline Staff*, which summarizes the causes of DID, the process of diagnosing the condition, and a treatment protocol that utilizes what we know about treating complex trauma and attachment wounds while providing adjustments to those treatments. However, what I have heard from therapists is that they need a shorter, more accessible "how-to" manual that they can immediately implement in their day-to-day practice—an easy-to-follow guide that answers their pressing questions and provides concrete suggestions for assisting clients with DID in establishing stability.

Having worked with dozens of clients with DID for more than thirty years, I have developed a set of best practices, comprising ten aspirations and three foundational pillars, for working with dissociative clients. By implementing the guidelines in this book, any therapist who is already skilled in working with clients with complex trauma can effectively work with clients with DID.

In order to assist readers in getting their bearings, **chapter 1** takes a deep dive into understanding identity and uncovers some biases widely held in the dominant culture of the United States. In **chapter 2**, I explore clinical considerations when diagnosing clients with dissociative disorders and review other diagnoses that have dissociation as possible symptoms. I also briefly review the diagnosis of other specified dissociative disorder (OSDD), as the best practices outlined in this book should be equally effective in working with clients diagnosed with OSDD. In fact, throughout the book, you can assume that any information or recommendations applied to clients with DID can be equally applied to those with OSDD.

---

of the United States in 2021 was 331.9 million, and 1.1%–3% of this population would be between 3.6 million and 10 million persons with DID. This is 18 to 50 times the number of cases to be considered rare. In spite of these data, the belief persists that DID is rare.

In **chapter 3**, I discuss the best practices for working with clients with DID by focusing on the ten aspirations involved in this process. The chapters that follow describe the three foundational pillars in detail,* as well as the three components of each pillar. **Chapter 4** focuses on the first pillar, *resourcing*, and its components: attunement, mindfulness/somatics, and imagination. **Chapter 5** describes the second pillar, *getting to know the alters*, and its components: introduction, roles, and internal world. Finally, **chapter 6** explains the third pillar, *the three Cs*, and its components: inner communication, cooperation, and co-consciousness** (Nooney, 2022; Schwarz et al., 2017; Steinberg & Schnall, 2001). When working with DID, I encourage you to use your own style and skill set while interweaving these three pillars into your work (see figure 1).

Figure 1: Best Practices for Working with DID

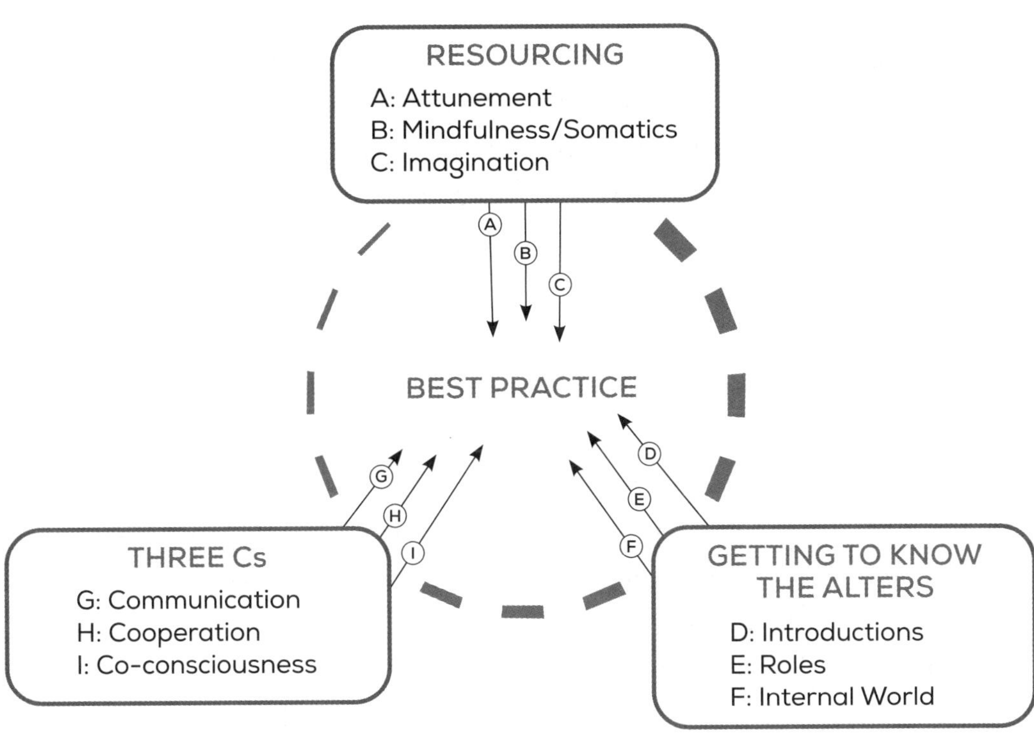

* The development of the three pillars has been influenced by the first three steps of an eleven-step stabilization treatment process proposed in *Diagnosing and Treating Dissociative Identity Disorder: A Guide for Social Workers and All Frontline Staff* (Nooney, 2022).

** Marlene Steinberg and Maxine Schnall (2001) based their recommended therapy for clients with dissociation on four Cs: comfort, communication, cooperation, and connection. In my view, Steinberg and Schnall's fourth C, *connection,* matches up with the third pillar's co-consciousness, and the first of their Cs, *comfort*, is comparable with the first pillar, *resourcing*.

In **chapter** 7, I describe in more depth the effects of developmental trauma and attachment wounds on clients with DID. Given that psychoeducation will be important for almost all clients with DID, **chapter 8** uses several client vignettes and sample dialogues to explore important areas of concern that clients often desire to understand better: diagnosis, dissociation, and the effect of trauma on brain functioning. **Chapter 9** covers a number of important issues that frequently come up when clients are faced with stressors in the outside world, including accommodations, safety, support systems, and frequent crises. **Chapter 10** shifts the focus back to the inner world and suggests helpful strategies for managing dissociation, including journaling and regular internal system meetings. Finally, in **chapter 11**, I provide suggestions as to how you can, in a practical and safe way, utilize tried and true bottom-up therapeutic strategies to help clients with DID process specific traumatic memories.

Due to the complexity of this work, I encourage you to seek out additional training and ongoing supervision when working with clients with DID. Equally important is that you be aware of the risks of countertransference, especially if you grew up in an environment characterized by insecure attachment. This work requires that you be fully present, curious, nonjudgmental, flexible, and emotionally stable. Although these attributes are necessary for any therapeutic work involving complex trauma and attachment wounds, they are especially important when working with clients with DID.

Above all, remember that clients with DID are people who experienced early childhood trauma and attachment wounds, and they developed creative dissociative strategies as a way to survive. The extent of their dissociation may be more extreme than clients with other diagnoses, as they have succeeded in creating distinct identities that can take over the body. While this can be frightening to some, what should be more frightening and concerning, in my view, is the abuse and neglect they experienced as children, which created the need for such dissociation in the first place.

It is time to welcome those with dissociative identities back into your clinics and consulting rooms. It is time to treat them with the respect they deserve and to honor their struggles. It is time to join with them in your therapeutic spaces to assist in their healing. With this introductory guide, you can begin to do so.

CHAPTER 1

IDENTITY

Before I delve into the details of diagnosing and working with clients with DID, it is important to reflect on what is meant by the idea of a *personal identity*. Until you understand this concept, you risk allowing your personal, cultural, or implicit biases to determine your perception of those with a dissociative identity.

As we move throughout our lives, our identities change in countless ways. I think about myself and define my identity today, at the age of seventy-three, quite differently than I did at the age of three, or twenty-three, or fifty-three. The atoms and cells in my body are not the same today as they were many decades ago, nor is my brain. My memories and worldview are different. Yet, I stubbornly hold on to the belief that there is a "me" who has somehow survived all these changes.

The belief that we all have a deeply rooted and unchanging self is widespread in Western culture. Many religious traditions define this concept as the *soul*. Unsurprisingly then, this idea of a "self" is prevalent within many of the psychotherapy models and approaches. For example, Lisa Schwarz and colleagues (2017) refer to this sense of unchanging identity as the "Core Self." Hal and Sidra Stone (1989) argue that all humans have multiple selves and that identifying and working with them is essential for wellness; they then redefine these selves as subpersonalities and insist that there is an essential self, based on our psychic imprint, called our "true being." In the Internal Family Systems (IFS) model, there is the recognition that while all humans have multiple parts, there still exists an innate presence called the "Self," which is the core of the individual and has qualities of compassion, confidence, creativity, courage, clarity, calmness, connectedness, and curiosity (Anderson et al., 2017). Arielle Schwartz (2021) has embraced this notion and referred to it as the "present-centered adult self."

When considering what the self means, we can also look to *Merriam-Webster*'s word of the year for 2023: *authentic*. To be authentic is to be true to ourselves, though the dictionary definition doesn't clarify what this "self" is to which we must be true. Grant Brenner (2023) argues that while it's important to be aware of the multiple aspects of ourselves, to be authentic is ultimately about being true to our core self or true self. Gabor Maté (2022), refers to the self as "one's own unique and genuine essence" (p. 106). Essentially, the dominant view in the culture of psychotherapy is that we all possess some version of an unchanging self deep within us, even if we may have some difficulty accessing it at times.

However, some therapeutic modalities disagree that our identity is founded on the existence of an unchanging core self. For example, Gestalt therapy has a more flexible concept of self that emphasizes the importance of living in the present moment while developing a constantly changing awareness of both the self and the outside world (Shorkey & Uebel, 2013). My interpretation is similar: that the self—rather than residing, unchanged, at the center of our existence—is instead subject to continual change. Veronica O'Keane (2021) disputes the notion of an unchanging self, noting that identity is synonymous with story. If there is no story, then there is no continuous sense of self. Our stories are, of course, perpetually in flux. Michael White (2007), the cofounder of narrative therapy, also believes our identity is not tied to an unchanging core self. Instead, he focuses on the multiple narratives that constitute our lives and emphasizes that there is no place to stand outside of story.

In my experience in working with clients with DID, I find it helpful to embrace this alternate view of the self as aligned with stories—richly or thinly described, but always changing. It frees me from thinking that there must be an original self, a host, a true self, or a core self, to which various other parts or alters are subservient. In order to be consistent with this view throughout this book, I will refer to the identity who fronts the client's body most of the time as the *primary* alter. This is often, but not always, the alter who takes responsibility for day-to-day decisions.

Letting go of the notion of a core self makes it easier for you to remain curious about how a particular client with DID may have created and structured their unique internal world and their system of alters. As new alters emerge during therapy, your curiosity will be in the forefront, and you will discover attributes of the alters, their particular roles in the system, and their unique skills and perspectives. You will be less likely to be distracted by preconceived notions about how your client's system "should" be organized, and you will be able to more easily step away from the therapist-defined role of the "expert."

Another problem with the concept of a core self is that it considers a singular identity to be the norm—the prerequisite for a healthy identity. With this viewpoint, a person with multiple identities is seen as abnormal, unhealthy, and pathological. The unquestioned result is that a singular identity with a core self is privileged over multiple identities. In my view, this is an example of implicit bias. If you accept this premise, then integrating all the alters into a single identity becomes the ultimate goal of therapy, or what is known as identity integration (ISSTD, 2011) or stable integration (Ross & Halpern, 2009).

The dangers of advocating such a fusion of alters are many. Alters who have experienced profound abandonment are stuck in the past, holding fast to those disturbing feelings in order to protect other parts of the system. It could be devastating and retraumatizing for them to hear you, their therapist whom they have slowly begun to trust, tell them that for therapy to be successful, they must cease to be themselves and somehow merge together with all the other parts of the system.

If there was evidence that clients with DID are unable to live productive, fulfilling lives unless they became a singular identity, then there could be a convincing argument for total integration of alters. However, I have found the opposite to be true in my clinical experience, where many clients have been able to move forward in their lives in a healthy manner while maintaining multiple identities.

Although it may be difficult for you to acknowledge and reject the implicit bias that privileges a singular identity over multiple identities, to do so fits well with the idea of encouraging client self-determination, trusting the process, and letting go of the outcome (Nooney, 2022).

MULTIPLICITY

The notion of multiplicity, that is, the idea that we're all made up of parts, is implicit in many well-known therapeutic approaches. For instance, dialectical behavior therapy (DBT) suggests that we all have an emotional mind and a rational mind, and they have the capacity to join together to create what is known as *wise mind*. Of course, this description of a three-part system has been oversimplified, but you can consider it a start in understanding multiplicity. Similarly, IFS considers that we all have an inner system of parts, composed of different kinds of parts called managers, firefighters, and exiles, that is led by the Self. Among therapists who work with trauma survivors, the interest in doing parts work has blossomed with the increasing popularity of IFS (Anderson, 2021).

One of the first times I recall thinking about myself as having parts was as I reflected on Stephen Fry's interpretation of the original *Star Trek* series (Allshorn, 2021). In this interpretation, Captain Kirk was the decision maker; Spock, who comes from a culture where logic is valued above all else, was the rational part; and McCoy, a down-to-earth doctor who cares for the crew's emotional and physical well-being, was the emotional part. Whenever an important decision needed to be made, Kirk consulted with Spock, who provided the logical solution, and with McCoy, who presented the emotional choice. Sometimes Kirk went with Spock's decision, and other times with McCoy's.

The practice of perceiving ourselves as having parts goes back much further than the *Star Trek* franchise, DBT, or IFS. For example, among Indigenous cultures, practitioners of Shamanic and Celtic healing arts, and Hindu and Buddhist mythologies, we have seen multiplicity present within the human psyche for hundreds of years (Marich, 2023). Recognizing multiplicity in medicine dates back at least to Antoine Despine's work in the 1830s, where we can find one of the first documented cases of the diagnosis and treatment of DID (Fine, 1988).

In current times, social media has created spaces where people have the ability to explore their internal parts with others. For example, the Plural Association is a peer-led organization formed to empower individuals with multiple parts. The Plural Association prefers the term *plurals* to describe those who identify as having parts, whether they meet the definition of DID or not. In fact, the organization opposes seeing multiplicity as pathological. When I work with clients who have been diagnosed with DID, I am eager to acknowledge that their alters came into existence through a creative act, designed specifically as an elegant method of survival. But even if we accept that we all have parts inside us, and that identifying and accepting those parts is helpful and healthy, this doesn't relieve us of the challenge of identifying those who meet criteria for DID and those who are close to it (such as those with OSDD).

No one knows yet how clients with DID develop the capacity to create and maintain multiple versions of their selves. We do, however, have some clues from neuroscience when we consider the role of the agranular prefrontal cortex (aPFC) and granular prefrontal cortex (gPFC) (Bennett, 2023). The aPFC is the most ancient of frontal regions and developed in the brains of our tiny mammalian ancestors way back in the time of the dinosaurs. The aPFC, along with the rest of the sensory neocortex region, provided those four-inch-long rat-like creatures with the ability to create a model of the external world, which greatly improved their ability to find their way into safe crevices to escape the larger and deadly reptiles.

Then with the emergence of the much newer gPFC, along with several new regions of the sensory neocortex—such as the temporoparietal junction and the superior temporal sulcus, which appears solely in humans and our primate cousins—something quite amazing happened. We developed the ability to model the model. In other words, we can create a model of ourselves. This enables metacognition, or the ability to think about our own thinking. The gPFC also allows us to create models of important persons in our lives. Whether they are still alive or have passed on, we maintain a model of our parents, siblings, friends, and other people who have influenced us. When I think of my wife, I still have a model of her in my gPFC, but I do not confuse the model with the reality of her. I know she exists outside of me, outside of my model of her. Similarly, when I think of my deceased mother, I can still pull up an image of her, but I know she is no longer with us. I do not confuse the model with the reality of her death.

Although we do not yet have sufficient data on the role of the gPFC in DID, I imagine that clients with DID are somehow able to use this structure as a place to store and replicate models of all the alters in their sophisticated systems. How these models are able to take on a life of their own, interact with each other, and construct an internal world that has a different kind of reality is still a mystery.

LANGUAGE AND TERMINOLOGY

Person-First Language vs. Identity-First Language

When working with clients with a diagnosis of DID, language and terminology can be challenging because of the medical model upon which insurance claims are based. In the United States, insurance companies routinely require therapists to justify the payment for therapeutic services by arguing that such services are medically necessary. As a result, it is common for therapists to talk about people as "schizophrenics" or "DID patients." To do so is disrespectful because it directs your focus onto the *condition* rather than the complexity of the person with whom you are working. There is also a real danger that clients might identify with the diagnosis. Therefore, it is important to use person-first language (e.g., "a person with schizophrenia" or "a person with DID"), which centers the person—not their diagnosis.

In order to create some distance from the medical model, I also encourage using the term *client* rather than *patient*, as the latter puts the therapist in a position of power over the client, in which they are the sole expert, and the patient is someone to be "fixed." Although the term *client* also has problems, as it may conjure up images of attorneys or accountants, until a better word can be suggested, I consider it preferable to *patient*.

Importantly, shifting the language you use to refer to your clients only takes you a short distance. If you speak of "treating" a client with DID, the implication is that you treat, while the client receives the treatment. This necessitates a therapist-centered interaction rather than a client-centered one. Doctors can medically treat a patient's broken arm, torn ligament, or heart condition. On the other hand, therapists work collaboratively with persons who are struggling with difficult life situations. But neither schizophrenia, depression, nor DID can be "medically treated" because none of these conditions can be pointed to, prodded, or touched.

The penetration of the medical model into the consulting room creates problems for all therapeutic work, but especially so with clients who have histories of complex trauma and whose healing requires the development of healthy agency and empowerment. One way to step away from these assumptions is to indicate that you are "working in therapy with a person who meets criteria for DID" or "working in therapy with a person who has been diagnosed with DID." Another possibility is to borrow from Jamie Marich (2023), who has suggested dropping the "disorder" language and instead saying "working collaboratively with a person with a dissociative identity."

Due to the length and awkwardness of such phrasing, it would be difficult to consistently utilize these language suggestions in a book format, so while I have attempted to avoid using the word *treat* to the extent possible, there are times I use them to avoid unwieldy or awkward phrasing. For simplicity's sake, I also refer to individuals who seek out therapy as "clients with DID."

Naming the Alters

Language and terminology also have an impact in how you refer to multiplicity. For example, sometimes it is clearer to use the word *system* rather than *client* when referring to the individual seeking therapy, but know that the terms are basically interchangeable since the client is a system of alters. To make things more complicated, alters can vary by gender, ethnicity, and sometimes even species—for example, a system can have an alter who identifies as an angel, a demon, an animal, or an inanimate object. Each alter may also use a different pronoun. How you refer to these separate states is not a neutral proposition. The best practice is to use whatever terminology the client prefers. There are many possibilities: friends, inner friends, aspects, parts, the littles, peeps, the others, or the people inside. For the purposes of this book, I will generally use the terms *parts* or *alters*, which is an abbreviation for *alternate identity*. If the alters have names, it is preferable to use their name when referring to them, as this supports agency and authentication.

Another problem you may run into is how to refer to the person who first comes in to therapy and who, for the most part, runs the show. Upon first meeting a client, you usually won't know that they have DID, so whatever name the client offers is the name that you should use. This is good practice with any new client; ask what they prefer to be called, as there are many people who don't like to be called by their given name or who prefer a nickname. This is especially important if you later discover the person has DID.

It is also a mistake to assume that a client's legal name is the name of the alter who attends the first therapy session. Likewise, do not surmise that the client's legal name is the name of the alter who is prominent in the system. There are many other possibilities:

1. There may be several alters who take turns being in charge (i.e., fronting the body).
2. The alter who almost always fronts the body may use the legal name as their name, but a different alter may front the body in the first meeting for various reasons. Perhaps the one who usually fronts the body didn't want to go to therapy, and the other alter took over to make sure they got to the appointment.
3. The alter who uses the legal name may not be the alter who usually fronts the body.

For all these reasons, it is a mistake to privilege the alter who uses the client's legal name as being the "real person" or the "host," and all the other alters as somehow "belonging to" the real person. Most of us feel disrespected if someone calls us by the wrong name, mispronounces our name, or uses the wrong pronouns in referring to us. Alters need to be granted the same respect. There is a notion in fantasy lore that if you know someone's true name, you have power over them. So perhaps not coincidentally, when you first meet an alter, they will sometimes be reluctant to reveal their name. Since alters reside in a sometimes-fantastical inner world, their reluctance might be related to a sense of not wanting to give up their power.

If an alter will not reveal their name, it could also be that they do not have one. In this case, you can encourage them to name themselves, which adds a degree of agency to their experience. Another possibility is to simply ask how they'd like you to refer to them. Sometimes they will reveal their age as a way to name them. For example, if they are seven years old, they may prefer "the seven-year-old" or just "Seven."

Sometimes an alter who has internalized feelings of self-hatred may tell you that their name is a vulgar term or something that would be harmful to call another person. In such a case, you may be concerned that addressing the alter with that name would make you complicit with their previous experiences of abuse. The solution to this dilemma is for you to explain your reasoning and to request a different way to refer to the alter. If the alter has no suggestions, you might ask the primary alter for an idea.

Clients may use the pronoun *we* to describe themselves. Doing so may be considered a positive development because it demonstrates an acceptance of their multiplicity. Some clients will also have alters with pronouns that differ from that of the primary. While it is certainly possible for a client with DID to be transgender or gender fluid, it is a mistake to assume that having mixed genders in the system means the client identifies as transgender. The best practice is to consult with clients and their particular alters as to which pronouns they use.

OUTSIDER KNOWLEDGE VS. INSIDER KNOWLEDGE

Like all humans, I have parts within myself, as do you. In order to be an effective therapist for clients with DID, it is essential that you be aware of any unresolved issues in your past that could potentially derail your attunement and effectiveness in working with clients. One way to do this is to do "parts work" with yourself and to consult regularly with your inner parts, especially whenever you're confronted with difficult emotional reactions while doing therapy. This awareness is not, however, enough to totally understand the experience of a client with DID, where the internal parts are significantly more defined. Only those clients have access to insider knowledge. Since I do not fit into those categories, I can only provide outsider knowledge.

The value of insider knowledge cannot be overstated, so I invite you to pay close attention to the information your clients provide to you. I also recommend you seek out other resources* offering insider information. An excellent place to start is the work of Jamie Marich, who has lived experience with dissociation. In her book *Dissociation Made Simple*, she integrates knowledge and information from more than sixty contributors who also have lived experience with dissociation, many of whom have been diagnosed with DID (Marich, 2023).

---

* I suggest the following resources for insider information on DID and multiplicity: *An Infinite Mind* (www.aninfinitemind.com); the website of Adrian Fletcher, PsyD (www.drfletch.com); *Beauty After Bruises* (www.beautyafterbruises.org); Dylan Crumpler's *Petals of a Rose* (www.dylancrumpler.com); *Mad in America* (www.madinamerica.com); *The Mighty* (www.themighty.com); Hearing Voices Network (www.hearing-voices.org); Sidran Institute (www.hhri.org/organisation/the-sidran-institute); and Dr. Emily Christensen's *System Speak* podcast (www.systemspeakcommunity.com).

CHAPTER 2

DIAGNOSTIC PROCESS

Dissociative experiences are common among clients, especially those who have experienced complex trauma and attachment wounds. In fact, disorganized attachment is a strong predictor of dissociation, with anywhere between 15–25 percent of clients with this attachment style having experienced dissociation (Ijzendoorn et al., 1999). What's more is that, besides DID and OSDD, at least a dozen diagnoses in the *Diagnostic and Statistical Manual of Mental Disorders* (*DSM*; American Psychiatric Association [APA], 2022) have dissociation listed as a possible symptom. This includes:

- Dissociative amnesia
- Depersonalization/derealization disorder
- Reactive attachment disorder
- Disinhibited social engagement disorder
- Acute distress disorder
- Posttraumatic stress disorder (PTSD)
- Bipolar I and bipolar II disorders
- Intermittent explosive disorder
- Substance-related disorders
- Neurocognitive disorders
- Borderline personality disorder (BPD)
- *Ataque de nervios*

As mentioned earlier, the *DSM* estimates that 1–1.5 percent of the population meets criteria for DID (APA, 2022), but the reality is that the condition is likely much more prevalent than is currently reported. That's because, unfortunately, many clients who meet criteria for DID are underdiagnosed or misdiagnosed, so they are only treated for co-occurring disorders that are easier to recognize (e.g., PTSD, BPD). However, until a client's DID diagnosis is acknowledged, treatment for any comorbid conditions is unlikely to be successful (APA, 2013).

Once you accept that DID is not rare, you will discover that the likelihood of encountering a client with this condition is high, especially if you work from a trauma lens and routinely encounter clients with early childhood trauma and attachment wounds. Therefore, it is imperative that you become comfortable in assessing the types and degrees of dissociation that your clients are experiencing in order to rule DID in or out.

When formulating a diagnosis, you need to remember that there is a hierarchical structure to many of the *DSM* diagnoses. For example, if you are working with a client who meets criteria for major depressive disorder (MDD), you cannot automatically give them that diagnosis without ruling out other conditions first. You would have to rule out persistent depressive disorder and bipolar I and bipolar II disorders first, as those disorders are higher in the hierarchy. If the client were to meet criteria for any of those diagnoses, then you would not diagnose MDD because all the criteria for MDD are contained within these other diagnoses. This is not simply an artifact of the *DSM*'s structure; it has important treatment implications as well. If you diagnose a client with MDD and they are prescribed an antidepressant without ruling out bipolar I disorder, the risk of an emerging manic episode becomes higher.

Similarly, if a client meets criteria for depersonalization/derealization disorder or dissociative amnesia, you would want to rule out DID first because the symptoms of these disorders will also be present in DID. If the client does in fact have DID, and you treat these other disorders with trauma-specific modalities without taking DID into consideration, retraumatization can occur, resulting in decompensation (see chapter 6).

Realistically, it may take a long time to make a definitive diagnosis of DID. While conducting a detailed inquiry of your client's experiences with childhood abuse and neglect might be helpful in coming up with a diagnosis, this is not recommended due to the risk of retraumatization. Even a discussion of dissociation can result in the opening of internal doors that have been carefully compartmentalized by clients with DID. In order to mitigate against increased retraumatization and disorganization, you must conduct such discussions slowly, at a pace that is acceptable for the client.

Among clients with a trauma history, you can often gather enough information to demonstrate that the client meets criteria for PTSD, and this diagnosis can remain as a placeholder if further exploration provides evidence that the client meets criteria for DID. The DSM doesn't preclude you from diagnosing certain anxiety or trauma-related disorders as co-occurring with DID, such as PTSD and panic disorder. In these cases, though, you should rule out DID prior to attempting to treat the comorbid disorder, especially if the client has early childhood trauma. Failing to do so can result in ineffective treatment or an increase in symptoms for those who do in fact have DID. The successful treatment of the DID will result in a reduction of the anxiety symptoms as well.

ASSESSMENT

An accurate diagnosis of a DID client requires a client to experience five types of dissociation: (1) dissociative amnesia, (2) depersonalization, (3) derealization, (4) identity alteration, and (5) identity confusion (van der Kolk et al., 2023). Since dissociative disorders are at least as common, and perhaps more common, than many other psychiatric disorders, the ISSTD (2011) recommends that every new client be assessed for these symptoms.

According to Bessel van der Kolk and colleagues (2023), you can begin by asking whether the client loses chunks of time (dissociative amnesia) and whether their body feels like it doesn't belong to them (depersonalization). If they cannot remember what happened during the lost time and if they don't feel their body belongs to them, this increases the likelihood of a DID diagnosis. In addition, you should ask clients whether they've ever had the experience of a familiar setting suddenly becoming radically unfamiliar (derealization), as well as whether they have experienced strangers recognizing them and claiming to know them—possibly even calling the client by a different name (identity alteration). Finally, you should ask the client whether they sometimes feel like they don't know who they are, as if they feel like they are another person (identity confusion).*

* Loewenstein (1991) recommends that you ask important questions regarding dissociation when doing a mental status exam, including inquiries about blackouts; disremembered behavior; fugues; unexplained possessions; inexplicable changes in relationships; fluctuations in skills, habits, and knowledge; fragmentary recall of history; chronic mistaken identity experiences; micro-dissociations; and autohypnotic symptoms.

Screening Questions

1. Can you tell me a little bit about how good your memory is currently?

   [Follow up by asking about lost blocks of time, including how curious the client is about discovering what happened during those times and whether they have ever ended up in trouble due to things they might have done during those times. In addition, ask whether the client has ever found themselves somewhere and not known how they got there.]

2. How about your history? Are there large gaps in your memory regarding your past?

   [Follow up by asking about important events that one would expect to be able to remember, such as early childhood memories, memories about going to school, or memories about places they have lived.]

3. Have you ever discovered something you own but can't remember purchasing it?

   [Follow up by inquiring about these possessions, including whether some have disappeared unexpectantly, such as clothing that the client wouldn't ever want to wear. In addition, ask about drawings or writings the client does not recall ever creating.]

4. How about your sense of self? Do you ever feel like you are not quite yourself? Like you are a different age, or you don't feel like yourself in your body?

   [Follow up by asking whether the client has experienced times when they have sensed that the world around them was different or unusual.]

5. Have you ever experienced major changes in your relationships with others and had no idea why it happened?

   [Follow up by asking whether client has experienced times when they've met people who insist they know the client—but the client doesn't recall ever meeting them—or people who call the client by a different name that the client has never used.]

6. Are you ever able to quite effectively block out physical pain?

   [Follow up by asking about having out-of-body experiences, spacing out, being on automatic pilot, or streaming through life without feeling they were actually present.]

7. Many people have an inner dialogue going on—for example, when they're planning a new activity—or an inner voice, like a conscience, that tells them right from wrong. Do you ever experience this?

   [Follow up by asking whether there is more than one distinct inner voice, whether inner voices ever talk to each other, whether there are any child voices, and whether the voices seem to have names.]

Given that most therapists now use electronic medical records (EMR), it is essential that these systems accommodate these important questions. Examine your EMR system to determine whether it allows you to record this data easily and regularly. If not, see if it's possible to make alterations to your system to ensure that this is the case.

Even though hearing voices is not a criterion for DID, clients with DID have alters who have the ability to communicate with the primary and with each other, so it is highly likely that they will have some experiences of hearing voices. If a client hears childlike voices or more than three voices, the likelihood of a DID diagnosis increases. Even so, they may not share this information with you out of fear that they will be diagnosed with schizophrenia. This fear is warranted, as between 25–50 percent of clients with DID have been mistakenly diagnosed with schizophrenia (Ross, 1999).

The following sample dialogue between a client and therapist illustrates some of the early discussions that are instructive to the diagnostic process. In this interaction, the subject of dissociation is discussed openly, which not only provides some helpful psychoeducation for the client but is also diagnostically valuable:

Therapist: It's good to see you again. How has your week gone?

Client: Okay, I guess. Same old, same old.

Therapist: Is there anything that has happened in your life that you wanted to talk about today?

Client: Not really. I have been wondering if you've figured me out yet. [*She smiles.*]

Therapist: I was hoping we could work together on that project.

Client: Yeah, sure.

Therapist: Do you remember how we talked a lot about your struggles with memory in our last session?

Client: No, I can't remember. [*She laughs.*]

Therapist: You got me! Seriously, though, would it be okay to talk a little more about it?

Client: Sure.

Therapist: Have you ever heard about a concept called dissociation?

Client: Sounds familiar, but I'm not sure.

Therapist: I bring it up because it fits with a discussion about memory. When a person dissociates, they sort of space out, and sometimes they don't remember what happened during that time.

Client: That happens all the time with me.

Therapist: Could you give me an example?

Client: When I'm doing the dishes or some other household chore, my husband might be talking to me, and I don't even hear him. Later, he tells me that I answered his question, but I have no memory of it at all. Sometimes, I think he makes it all up so he can get away with something.

Therapist: That sounds like a good example of what I'm talking about—that is, unless your suspicion that your husband is making it up is true.

Client: To tell you the truth, it happens a lot, so I doubt he's making it up.

Therapist: Would it be fair to say that when this happens, you have lost a block of time?

Client: I never thought of it like that, but yeah, I guess that would be accurate.

Therapist: Has it ever happened to you with anyone besides your husband?

Client: [*She pauses.*] Come to think of it, it happened just the other day. My daughter suggested we go grocery shopping. I agreed and we got in the car. The next thing I knew, we were back home unpacking the groceries. I still can't remember going to the store. I didn't think much about it. Talking about it now though, it seems kind of weird. Huh.

At this point in the session, the therapist might provide more psychoeducation about dissociation. It would also be a good time to introduce the Dissociative Experiences Scale, which I discuss in greater detail in the following section, and to ask the client if they would be willing to fill it out. You could give the client the option of filling it out in session or at home. In either case, going over the items with a high score will provide additional examples that will help in the diagnostic process.

DISSOCIATIVE EXPERIENCES SCALE (DES-II)

The right screening questions are vital to begin the process of assessing for dissociation, but unfortunately, therapists are often not trained to ask them (Ross & Halpern, 2009). And even if you ask the right questions, many clients are still reluctant to share their dissociative experiences due to a lack of trust (Schwarz et al., 2017), as clients with DID are often misunderstood, stereotyped, and marginalized. In fact, it is estimated that only 6 percent of clients with DID will make their condition obvious (Kluft, 2009). To help you overcome this barrier, there are a number of useful screening instruments, many of which are open source and available on the ISSTD website at www.isst-d.org.

One of the easiest and most helpful screening tools is the Dissociative Experiences Scale (DES-II; Carlson & Putnam, 1993) for adults, or the Adolescent Dissociative Experiences Scale (A-DES; Armstrong et al., 1997) for children ages eleven to seventeen. The DES-II contains twenty-eight questions regarding dissociation that ask clients to note the percentage of time they have had particular experiences while not under the influence of alcohol or drugs. It is scored simply by adding up the responses and dividing by twenty-eight to get the average. Clients with DID often score above 40, but any score over 20 suggests further diagnostic assessment.

As a note, this instrument should not be used alone to diagnose DID; it is merely a screening tool. Another valuable use of this instrument is to interview the client after they have completed the instrument and to ask them to give examples for any items they rated at 20 percent or higher. Their answers are likely to provide a wealth of information about their current experiences with dissociation without the pressure of talking about traumatic events.

DIFFERENTIAL DIAGNOSIS

Posttraumatic Stress Disorder

Most clients with DID also meet criteria for PTSD, as many of the identifiable symptoms are the same, including intrusion, avoidance, and negative alterations of cognition, mood, arousal, and reactivity. However, in the intrusion category, dissociation is only one of five possible symptom clusters—and a diagnosis only requires that a client meet one of the five—so a person can meet criteria for PTSD even if they have no dissociative symptoms. For those who do dissociate, the typical type of dissociation is experienced as flashbacks. Clients who meet criteria for DID, on the other hand, will experience many different forms of dissociation not limited to flashbacks, including, as mentioned earlier, dissociative amnesia, depersonalization, derealization, identity alteration, and identity confusion.

For clients with PTSD who do not meet criteria for DID, their symptoms can best be described as extreme emotion dysregulation in which clients are unable to manage the intensity, frequency, or duration of their emotions. This dysregulation is triggered by any stimuli that remind the client of the trauma they have experienced, including external stimuli (e.g., sensory cues) and internal stimuli (e.g., certain thoughts, emotions, or sensations). In contrast, for those with DID, what may appear to be emotion dysregulation is actually a manifestation of the switching of alters, since each alter has their own unique personality traits and emotional intensities.

One other difference between PTSD and DID is that a diagnosis of PTSD requires the presence of at least one specific traumatic event where the client faced serious injury, sexual violence, or death. Since the identity fragmentation in DID is caused by such trauma in early childhood, these criteria would most likely also be met, but for many with DID, the specificity of such memories is unavailable to the client, at least in the beginning stages of therapy. Even if these memories are available, the client may not feel safe enough to reveal them. However, since many clients with DID have also experienced traumatic events in adulthood—which are often more easily accessible than childhood memories—a diagnosis of PTSD can often be made based on such a traumatic event.

As discussed earlier, if your client meets criteria for PTSD, you can make this diagnosis while engaging in further exploration of dissociative symptoms, making sure to also address the pertinent issues the client wishes to explore, such as the identification of triggers, interpersonal conflicts, and emotion dysregulation. As the therapeutic relationship strengthens, and if it becomes clear that the client has a system of identifiable alters, you can add the diagnosis of DID as appropriate.

Other Specified Dissociative Disorder

There are situations where there are identifiable alters in the client system, but the dissociative barriers between those parts are less rigid than one might expect in a client with DID. As a result, the inner communication and cooperation is already pretty well established, and there is much less amnesia. In such a case, a diagnosis of OSDD may be appropriate. OSDD may also be appropriate when you are not sure whether criteria for DID has been met, or if you are working with a client who is not ready to accept the diagnosis of DID. Whether or not your client has DID or OSDD, remember that the ten aspirations and three pillars presented in this book are appropriate for clients with either diagnosis.

Borderline Personality Disorder

Clients with BPD exhibit difficulties with emotional reactivity, interpersonal conflicts, and identity disturbances, especially under times of stress. These identity disturbances in particular are often characterized by episodes of dissociation in which a client may feel like they are in a trance, detached from their body, or running on autopilot. It is estimated that as many as 64 percent of clients with BPD exhibit some sort of dissociative symptoms (Sar et al., 2003). However, these episodes tend to be short-lived and occur in response to feeling abandoned, as opposed to the frequent and diagnostically significant amount of dissociation experienced by clients with DID.

Given the overlapping dissociative symptoms in BPD and DID, it is likely that a significant number of clients who have been diagnosed with BPD meet criteria for DID as well (ISSTD, 2011), with estimates ranging as high as 11 percent (Conklin & Westen,

2005). However, it is important to remember that according to the *DSM*, if the symptoms of any personality disorder are better explained by another mental disorder, then a personality disorder should not be diagnosed. Since clients with DID often have alters who take charge of the body, a clinician could easily interpret an alter's actions as pathological personality traits assigned to those with BPD, such as emotional lability, anxiousness, separation insecurity, depressivity, impulsivity, risk-taking, and hostility. However, if the client meets criteria for DID, and the symptoms of DID better explain these symptoms, then neither BPD nor any other personality disorders should be diagnosed.

Ultimately, diagnosis is a delicate process that requires sensitivity, nuance, and skill to accurately tease apart the symptoms leading to a client's distress. As therapy progresses and more diagnostic information is gradually gleaned, the diagnosis will often change. For example, a client may initially meet criteria for PTSD, but as the extent of dissociation is discovered, OSDD may be more appropriate, finally leading to a DID diagnosis. The common thread here is the early childhood trauma and attachment wounds that these clients experience.

CHAPTER 3

ASPIRATIONS

In this book, I define three foundational pillars that are crucial for effectively working with clients with DID—resourcing, getting to know the alters, and the three Cs—which are so crucial that they can be considered best practices. As I have considered these practices in my work over a period of four decades, I have concluded that they cannot stand alone. Otherwise, a therapist's worldview, values, and implicit biases will inevitably influence the effectiveness of these foundational pillars.

In chapter 1, I outlined two such biases that pose a potential threat: the idea of the singular core self and the medical model. As you examine your own most cherished principles and beliefs, as well as those that are endemic in the dominant culture and the culture of psychotherapy, you may uncover others that are equally relevant.

When we fall back on unconscious biases such as these, it has "the potential to restrict us to the unquestioned reproduction of what is familiar in terms of therapeutic practice, regardless of the consequences on the lives of the people who consult us" (White, 2007, p. 6). To reduce the hazards of remaining unconscious, I am proposing ten aspirations for you to consider as you move forward with learning and implementing the three pillars. Although you may find that some of the aspirations easily fit with your therapeutic posture, others might be more difficult to adopt. For this reason, I call them aspirations rather than commitments, principles, or ground rules.

These aspirations have been a focus and a challenge for me throughout my career, but I also want to acknowledge that they are not etched in stone as the only aspirations you might find important in your therapeutic work with dissociative clients. By the time this book is published, I might discover other aspirations that I could easily include in this list. My hope is that you will spend some time and energy stepping into these aspirations and consider how consciously adopting them into your practice might improve your work. At the same time, by developing a practice of exploring your own unique principles and values, you might enhance your own understanding of yourself and your clients.

ASPIRATIONS

1. Remember that your client has crucial "insider knowledge," whereas you only possess "outsider knowledge."
2. Remind yourself that your client is the whole system, not any particular alter.
3. Center the client system in therapy rather than yourself as the expert.
4. Foster an abundance of curiosity regarding the client's system.
5. Be congruent in your presentation with courageous honesty and transparency.
6. Have the courage to enter your client's inner realm while always staying grounded in this realm.
7. Trust the process rather than focusing on your expectations for the outcome.
8. Be acutely aware of your own limitations and share with your client when appropriate.
9. Seek out consultation and your own personal therapy when needed, especially when experiencing countertransference.
10. Remind yourself that prior to your client meeting you, they have very likely lived through and survived much worse experiences than they are having now.

Before you read through each aspiration in more detail, I would be remiss if I didn't first mention a rock-hard principle that undergirds them, and which is as true for working with clients with DID as with any other client: Follow your own discipline's code of ethics and all legal requirements.

1. Remember that your client has crucial "insider knowledge," whereas you only possess "outsider knowledge."

As discussed in chapter 1, your clients, no matter how disorganized and dysregulated they are, have insider information that you, as the therapist, do not possess. An important part of your job is to facilitate them in accessing that information for healing. The key here is humility. By necessity, you will often provide psychoeducation for your clients. While pursuing the three pillars, you will also be asking lots of questions. Especially once you have developed some skill and success in working with clients with DID, you may find yourself exaggerating the importance of your outsider knowledge.

In my experience, significant growth and healing happen when a new idea, strategy, or creative idea leads to a change in the client's experience, and these almost always come from their own inner world. As the therapist, it is important to be curious about a client's system (aspiration 4), but it is even more important when the client becomes genuinely curious about their own system. They can then adapt and carry out into the world their newfound insider knowledge.

2. Remind yourself that your client is the whole system, not any particular alter.

In working with a client with DID, you may find yourself liking one alter more than others. For example, with many clients, the primary alter is the first alter you meet, and you may have established attunement and a therapeutic relationship with that alter prior to diagnosing DID. As other alters are identified in the system, it would be easy to think of the primary alter as your client, and the other alters as less important. To further complicate this issue, the primary alter may insist they are the "real person," and they may have a conflictual relationship with some of the other alters. In fact, some of those alters might insult or put down the primary, and you may have an impulse to protect the primary.

Once you realize this is happening, it is imperative that you remind yourself that the primary is also an alter, and that every alter, no matter how they are behaving, is an important part of the system. You must be aware that your client is the whole system. Otherwise, you can easily get caught taking sides in alter conflicts. The third pillar, the three Cs, is about helping all the alters learn to connect with each other and resolve their conflicts. When you take sides, you become a hindrance to those goals.

Every alter has an important role in the system and needs to be honored and respected. Very likely, there will be alters who are too angry or rageful to be allowed to front the body, and there may be alters who are hidden away or exiled in cages, caves, or other structures. Acknowledging that an alter is too dangerous to be allowed to front the body does not mean that it is okay to reject or diminish that alter. They helped the client survive abuse and neglect at one or more points in the past. To reject them is to reproduce that abuse and neglect. Some alters may reject other alters, but it is important that you do not fall into that trap. Rather, it is important to remind your client that they are now in a very different place than when they were subjected to the abuse and neglect. Often, the dangerous alters are unaware of all the changes that have occurred, as they may be stuck in the past. You can encourage other alters in the system to find ways to reeducate the dangerous alters so they can find new roles that serve the system.

I will discuss this topic in more detail in chapter 5, especially in the section entitled *Internal Worlds.*

3. Center the client system in therapy rather than centering yourself as the expert.

This principle is especially helpful when, over the course of therapy, the client engages in destructive behavior or presents dilemmas that have no perceivable solution. For example, the client might begin a session by discussing a conflict they have with a spouse, family member, business associate, or friend. At first, you might engage in some problem-solving discussion, helping the client gain a wider perspective of the conflict and consider various solutions. Due to the trauma cycle, which you will learn about in chapter 7, solutions to the particular conflict or dilemma are likely to fail. This is because the power of the trauma cycle is stronger than any reasonable solution.

There are two shifts in perspective that will help you as you strive to embrace this aspiration. First, remind yourself that your client is the system (aspiration 2), not the particular alter who presented the problem to you. Other alters very likely have possible solutions that you and the alter with whom you are meeting would not have considered. Second, step away from offering options that might lead to a resolution of the conflict or dilemma. This is a crucial additional step: stop centering yourself as the expert who might have some good ideas for resolution.

Once you have successfully made these shifts, the focus of the session immediately changes to a deeper involvement of the second pillar, getting to know the alters, and the third pillar, the three Cs. Sometimes, this alone will result in the client coming up with some solutions to try. If not, you can always suggest that they continue to consult with the others in between sessions and see what they can come up with, possibly utilizing journaling or resourcing on their own.

4. Foster an abundance of curiosity regarding the client's system.

As you experience the world, you are bombarded by more sensory information than your brain can effectively process. As a workaround, you use your memories to pull up well-constructed models or schemas of what you expect to find, but some of what you experience will be different from your preconceived schema. In turn, your attention will be drawn to those bits of data so your brain can make adjustments to the schema. As a result, curiosity emerges. In this respect, neuroscientist Charan Ranganath (2024) concludes that curiosity is intrinsically connected to memory. You are compelled, then, to ask questions as a way to explore those novel differences. Ranganath's work, however, does not provide clues as to what those questions might be when you are working with a client.

The particular questions you ask are influenced by what you have learned from your particular discipline, from the workshops you have attended, and from the books and articles you have read. In addition, you are significantly influenced by the overall dominant culture, the medical model, the expectations of insurance companies, the pathological orientation of the *DSM*, and the culture of psychotherapy, where normalizing judgments are privileged. Since there are an infinite number of possible questions you can ask when working with clients (White, 2007), it is impossible to point to one question as the *right question* in any given situation. However, there are in fact *wrong questions*. A wrong question would be one that reflects your curiosity about something that, even as a therapist, is none of your business or that is likely to shift the sense of agency from the client to you. One way to reduce the chances of that happening is to, as Alice Morgan (2000) suggests, only ask questions to which you genuinely do not know the answer.

This advice is helpful for all clients. In reference to clients with DID, it is important to remember that every client system is unique, so you must withhold judgment as to how each client's system is organized and structured. Although it can be tempting to embrace various theories about how dissociative client systems are commonly structured, this is counterproductive for three reasons. First, there is an inherent power differential in the therapist-client relationship. That means if you propose a structure of the client's internal system that doesn't fit their experience, they might be reluctant to disagree with you and may become less engaged in the therapy process as a result. Second, the client might disregard their own knowledge and understanding of their inner world, leading them to adopt your frame of reference instead. This is disempowering for the client and could easily foster overdependence on your points of view. Third, the situation might result in inner conflict among the alters, with some wishing to be compliant with your point of view, others wanting to challenge you, and still others wanting to quit therapy.

For example, let's say you have a preconceived idea that a client system must have at least one protector alter and several child alters—a notion based on the types of schemas stored in your memory. Your client starts telling you about an alter named Peter. The existence of Peter, as an unknown alter, is a novel piece of information, so it would be natural for you to be curious about him and inquire further. A *wrong* question in this case might be "Is Peter your protector or is he a child?" This is a closed-ended question that gives the client only two options, and closed-ended questions are generally more prone to biases than open-ended ones. In addition, the question reveals your bias toward how you believe the client's internal system must be constructed.

To avoid these pitfalls, before asking a question, first reflect on whether you think you already know what the correct answer should be. If you do, it is time to rephrase the question or pursue a different line of inquiry. For example, in the case of the alter named Peter, a possible alternative question to ask is "Would you be willing to tell me more about Peter?" You have no idea how the client might answer this question, so it is much easier to hold on to the abundance of curiosity that this aspiration suggests. Second, ask yourself why you want to know the answer to the particular question you are asking. What has stimulated your curiosity about this topic? Is your curiosity tainted by judgmentalism or a particular bias of yours? If you have succeeded in setting aside your tendency to judge, then consider whether the question is likely to move you and the client forward toward your mutually agreed on goals.

I must admit that automatically adopting my three-pillar proposal as a best practice is another example of a form of bias. To mitigate against the dangers of this, it is important to first get the client's buy-in for a DID diagnosis. Generally, some of this may have already taken place during the diagnostic process. Prior to focusing on the first pillar (resourcing), you will have already provided enough psychoeducation to make sure you have informed consent to do so. And unless the client acknowledges that they are part of a system that contains parts, it makes no sense to focus on the second pillar (getting to know the alters) or the third pillar (the three Cs).

If you are convinced DID is the correct diagnosis and the alter with whom you are speaking does not agree, you can still remain curious about the client's system: how it is structured, who are the alters who inhabit it, and what the alters' roles are in the system. Without arguing or contradicting the alter with whom you are speaking, you can provide historical information that led you to believe that they are part of a system. For example, you might note that during the previous session, you spoke with a different alter, and ask the client if they remember that.

In this work, there will always be paradoxes. Alters will have gaps in their memories and their understandings. The central theme of this aspiration is to steer your curiosity toward an openness in learning about the client's system without preconceived ideas.

5. Be congruent in your presentation with courageous honesty and transparency.

As you engage effectively in your therapeutic work, a close connection will develop between yourself and the client. However, due to the power differential in the relationship—after all, they are paying you and you potentially have the power to lock them up—the client will be especially attuned to your facial expression, posture, and tone of voice. Although this is true of all clients, it is particularly the case for those who have suffered early childhood trauma, including those with DID, who are keenly aware when there is a misfit between someone's facial expression, someone's tone of voice, and the content of the verbal exchange. These differences can be referred to as *incongruence.* For many of these clients, experiences of incongruence are associated with danger. For example, an abuser from the client's past might have claimed that they were beating the client because they love them.

In traditional psychoanalysis, therapists are encouraged to maintain an objective stance and not react to how the client presents themselves or what they say. Maintaining such a stance is not helpful in working with a client with DID, as they will sense that you are hiding your true feelings and will interpret this as insincerity. If your words do not align with your facial expression, tone of voice, and posture, your client will notice this. Even if the alter who is fronting the body doesn't notice the incongruence, there will likely be other alters listening and watching who will. This interferes with your ability to develop trust and achieve attunement, which, as you will read in chapter 4, is essential for positive outcomes.

However, you will likely have some sessions where the material discussed will resonate with you in ways that have the potential for countertransference. When this occurs, you must be able to compartmentalize your emotional reactions and commit to addressing these issues on your own at a later time. If you attempt to make these inner adjustments in the midst of a difficult session, you may overestimate your ability to remain transparent. This is when courageous honesty becomes paramount.

For example, let's say you are working with a client who describes a past traumatic experience that reminds you of a memory from your own childhood. In response, you unconsciously shift in your chair and your face shows signs of shock and pain. You quickly become aware of your own reaction and take a breath, while setting aside the memory and letting your own inner child know that you will tend to it later. You then shift your focus on the client and realize that the client has paused. You're don't know if the client was aware of your reaction, but in case they were, you share a little about your own reaction. You might say, "Wow! Thanks for sharing. I really felt the intensity of that memory." If this comment results in additional questions from the client, it is important to remain focused on the client's responses and to be as transparent as you can without overwhelming the client with your own self-disclosure.

6. Have the courage to enter the client's inner realm while always staying grounded in this realm.

Regardless of your religious or spiritual beliefs or non-beliefs, there are dimensions to this work that are different from the "normal" stressors of day-to-day life. Things will happen in the therapy room that will seem magical and otherworldly. Your client will not levitate or grow wings, but you might encounter alters who believe they have wings. Alters can turn into walls, memories can float around like billiard balls, and healing can happen unexpectedly as alters connect, disconnect, and share energy with each other. We have all experienced strange happenings when we are dreaming, so there is a deep part of us who understands the potentialities of the inner realms. These realms are as real to the client system as anything in the outside world.

As therapists, we cannot directly experience the inner worlds of our clients, but as they describe what is happening, with courage, we can allow ourselves to begin to feel the energies involved. At the same time, we have a responsibility to not get too consumed by those alternate realities. Changes that occur in the inner realms of a client's system will have direct effects on the way that client interacts in the physical world, but one or more alters must front the body and negotiate the difficulties this world offers. Even when we travel with a client in those other realms, we have a responsibility to keep one foot in this realm—to stay grounded—so we can check in with the client as to how those negotiations are progressing.

7. Trust the process rather than focusing on your expectations for the outcome.

Most therapists who have had positive experiences in doing inner child work, ego-state work, or other bottom-up therapeutic techniques—such as brainspotting (Grand, 2013), somatic archaeology (Gibson, 2008), eye movement desensitization and reprocessing (EMDR; Shapiro & Forrest, 2016), the comprehensive resource model (CRM; Schwarz et al., 2017), or IFS (Anderson, 2021; Anderson & Sweezy, 2016)—have witnessed the powerful healing that can take place in the lives of their clients. Therapists doing this work can also tell you that the timing and intensity of this work, the details regarding the memories that are activated, and the client's sensory experiences, remain out of their control. As a result, therapists doing this work have to let go of expectations and trust the process, knowing that a client's inner world has unique wisdom that the therapist does not possess.

When working with clients with DID, this inner world is laid bare in front of us without the supportive structure of a specific evidence-based modality that we can use to address it, like EMDR or IFS. This is a delightful and scary experience at the same time. In order to focus on the delightful, the key is to let go of any expectations for the outcome and to trust the process as you would with a more structured bottom-up therapy. Chapters 4 through 6 discuss this process in more detail.

8. Be acutely aware of your own limitations and share with your client when appropriate.

One of the things I have learned from Michael White (2007) is that when working with clients, it is important to set limits rather than boundaries. I think this is especially the case when working with clients with DID, as focusing on the language of "boundaries" can easily lead to experiences defined as "boundary violations," which, when discussed with clients, will often come across as an accusation.

For example, let's say you tell a client that one of your boundaries is to keep therapeutic interactions to business hours only and that you will not engage with clients in the evenings. This client says they understand and accept this boundary. You then get a call at 10:00 p.m. from a psychiatrist you work closely with in the emergency department of the local hospital. The psychiatrist says they have been assessing your client and would appreciate it if you would speak with the client on the phone, which you agree to do. As a result, your boundary has been *crossed* or *violated.*

On the other hand, when you talk to your clients about your limitations, you are honestly sharing something about yourself that has an impact on the relationship. For example, you can inform your client that you have limits of time and energy and that, as a result, you need to spend time with your family and relax and rejuvenate in the evenings. You would then help the client establish other resources they can use during those times if they were to be in crisis. If you decide to respond to the emergency department call, then this cannot be interpreted as a boundary violation.

Another example involves physical touch or romantic or sexual boundaries. If you explain to a client that you have a firm boundary around these issues, and the client develops romantic feelings toward you and ends up acting in a flirtatious way, you might accuse them of a boundary violation. On the other hand, if you explain your ethical limits regarding romantic involvement with clients, and the client acts in a flirtatious way, then you only need remind them of your ethical limits. In either case, the result is the same in that you engage the client in a conversation about their behavior. In the first case, you end up accusing the client of a boundary violation, leading to feelings of blame and shame. In the second case, you don't blame the client but simply explain again the limits imposed by your ethical commitments. The onus isn't on the client for doing something wrong, but on your commitment to ethics.

9. Seek out consultation and your own personal therapy when needed, especially when experiencing countertransference.

Clients with DID, by definition, have experienced early childhood trauma and attachment wounds. There will be times when they want to share some of these memories with you. If you have an open heart when listening to these stories, you will, to some extent, experience vicarious trauma. Whether that turns into secondary traumatic stress and compassion fatigue will depend on a number of factors, and there are no certainties.

One salient factor will be whether you were blessed with a secure attachment status when growing up or, if not, how far along you are in working through your own trauma and establishing an *earned secure life narrative.** Even with such protective factors, there will still be situations where you will get triggered. Perhaps the client shares their experience of being abused at the age of eight. If you had some traumatic experiences at that same age, those memories might unexpectedly pop up for you. If you have a child around that age and are struggling with parenting, those issues might emerge into your mind without warning. When such situations occur, it will be challenging to continue with the conversation.

Your responsibility at this point is, of course, to continue to focus on the client's needs. You must have the skill of setting aside your need to address your own unresolved trauma without doing harm to yourself. One way to do this is to "put the issue on a shelf" somewhere in your mind and make a commitment to address it later. Alternatively, if you are comfortable with parts work, you can quickly communicate with your younger part and let them know you are busy at the moment with something important but you will get back to them soon. Even if you are highly skilled in these strategies, it will still take at least a few moments to accomplish these steps. While engaged in your own internal processes, your client might very well notice you were distracted. This is when being honest and transparent (aspiration 5) comes to play. You must be straightforward about your distraction without overwhelming the client with your problems.

Once you have reestablished your focus and attunement with your client, you will get through the session as best you can. Then, as mentioned above, it is important that you follow through with your commitment to address this issue on your own. It will be helpful if you have a contingency plan already in place to seek consultation from a peer or supervisor whenever you find that you need additional assistance to handle your countertransference. For more intense situations, there may be times when you need to seek therapy for yourself.

10. Remind yourself that prior to your client meeting you, they have very likely lived through and survived much worse experiences than they are having now.

This last aspiration is designed to allow you to pause for a moment and regroup. There will inevitably be times when you will find yourself caught in a tragic set of circumstances with

* For a more detailed understanding of what an earned secure life narrative is, and how one achieves it, see "Interpersonal Neurobiology and Attachment" from the *Encyclopedia of Social Work* (Montgomery, 2020).

a client you care about. You will want desperately to do something to ease your client's pain. You will try every strategy and every modality that you know. You may even go round and round through the three pillars, and nothing will help.

My only suggestion for you when this occurs is to remind yourself of this aspiration. Your client has survived worse without your help. It is likely, if you let go, that they will also survive this situation. At any rate, you will be there for them as they struggle through it.

CHAPTER 4

RESOURCING: THE FIRST PILLAR

The importance of the first pillar, resourcing, cannot be understated. As with other survivors of early childhood trauma and attachment wounds, clients with DID have overly sensitive limbic systems, which leads them to perceive danger when there is none and to exaggerate danger when it is there. As a result, it is common for clients with DID to experience ongoing trauma and troublesome relationships, which results in chaotic lives.

Resourcing is an excellent tool to quiet the limbic system and assist clients in extricating themselves from their chaotic experiences. In fact, you can think of resourcing as "limbic system therapy" (van der Kolk, 2014). Although you can use whatever resourcing techniques you have in your repertoire when working with DID, there are three primary categories that I will explore here: (1) attunement, (2) mindfulness/somatics, and (3) imagination. If a client doesn't find one particular type of resourcing to be helpful, you can easily shift to a different category. Ultimately, it will be up to the individual alters in the client system to decide what types of resourcing are most effective.

ATTUNEMENT

Perhaps the most powerful type of resourcing is attunement, given that "the therapeutic alliance is the cornerstone of all treatment" (van der Kolk et al., 1996, p. 430), and this alliance can only occur if the client develops a secure attachment to you. You can conceptualize the attunement process as follows: First, you work to connect with the client and the client connects to you. However, since many clients with DID have experienced attachment wounds in early childhood or have had negative experiences with other medical professionals, it is understandably difficult for them to trust you. For these reasons, it is imperative that you bring an attitude of patience to this process, giving clients enough time to gradually develop this trust so that the crucial resource of attunement can be refined. Daniel Siegel (2011) describes this connection as a brain-to-brain sharing of energy and information.

Second, you must be skillful in attuning with your own internal parts so that you can be effective in helping your client discover, accept, and cooperate with their system and all the alters within it. If your ability to internally attune to your own system breaks down, you can experience countertransference that interferes with the therapeutic work. For example, consider a client who is beginning to interact with a child alter who experienced a particular form of physical abuse. As you work with this client, a memory from your own past emerges that is similar to the client's experience. In other words, your own eight-year-old inner child demands attention in the middle of the session. You must have the skills to resource yourself in this situation so you can continue to focus on your client. You might recall that this reflects aspiration 5: "Be congruent in your presentation with courageous honesty and transparency." If this issue continues, you must have the wherewithal to take responsibility to seek out peer consultation, your own therapy, or some other effective method of your choosing.

Attuning with the client's internal system is more challenging, and it will not occur quickly or all at once. Rather, it will be an integral part of the work throughout the therapy process. (The third pillar—the three Cs—is laser focused on this process.) Establishing attunement with a client with DID is especially challenging because of the many alters involved in the client's system, each with their unique experiences of trauma and their own perceptions of the world and the therapy process. Consequently, your job is to seek some kind of alliance or agreement with any internal alters who may be uneasy about the process (Nooney, 2023).

As you begin to do so, aspiration 4 becomes especially salient: "Foster an abundance of curiosity regarding the client's system." Listening nonjudgmentally to the client's story with genuine curiosity and setting aside preconceived notions as to how their particular system is organized will do much to help create that attunement. If you approach a client with DID with any preconceived notions as to how their system or internal world is organized, this is likely to be off-putting and interfere with the development of a strong therapeutic relationship. Remember that each client's system is organized in its own way, with its own unique unpredictable internal world. Stay genuinely curious and ask appropriate questions that you do not know the answers to.

MINDFULNESS/SOMATICS

Mindfulness and somatic work, which can include conscious breathing and meditative practices, are powerful resourcing tools because they incorporate bodily awareness and connection. Ideally, these practices allow the client's parasympathetic system to downregulate, helping the client feel calmer and making it easier for them to do the therapeutic work involved in the other two pillars: getting to know the alters and the three Cs. Unfortunately, for a client with DID, it is often more complicated than that.

Clients who dissociate do so by disconnecting from their bodies. That's because their traumatic memories often end up stored as physical sensations in the body, called *body memories*, instead of through the normal functioning of the hippocampus. These somatosensory experiences can be visual images that keep returning, unelicited, to the client, or physical sensations that tend to get stuck in various places in the body (van der Kolk, 1994). Even if the client is aware of these sensations, they are often unable to identity a connection between these sensations and the past traumatic experience.

This creates a dilemma for the therapeutic work. In order to heal from the effects of traumatic memories and the meaning the client ascribes to those memories, it is necessary to access them. One such entry point is the body, and this is where conscious breathing techniques come in. At its core, conscious breathing is the first step in achieving interoception—that is, an acute awareness of the sensations experienced in the body. Simply bringing awareness to the breath can bridge the mind and body connection. You may start with whatever breathing techniques you are already comfortable with. I like to start with conscious breathing, letting the client know that I will be breathing with them. I then invite the client to breathe normally (eyes closed or open, depending on their preference) but to be totally aware of their inhalation and their exhalation. If they are successful with this practice, I will then add other components, such as Earth breathing, where they imagine pulling in air from deep in the Earth, then exhaling all their distress back into the Earth. It is helpful to have a repertoire of breathing techniques, as clients will probably find some easy and others more difficult.

As a note, it is sometimes difficult for clients with DID to do even the simplest of breathing techniques. As soon as they begin the process of noticing their breath, their awareness drops down into the body. As they begin to feel body sensations that they have been working hard to suppress, this may activate emotional distress connected to certain body memories. This can lead some protective alters to feel the need to stop the process. If clients are initially unable to do any kind of breathing exercises, you can attempt various other mindfulness methods. One of simplest is called *present timing*, as illustrated in the following dialogue:

Therapist: What number would you put your anxiety right now on a scale of 0 to 10?

Client: Probably a 6.

Therapist: I was wondering if you would be willing to do some conscious breathing as a way to calm yourself. I will do it with you.

Client: I'll try, but I don't think it will work.

Therapist: Okay, it might be easier if you close your eyes, but it's okay to keep them open if you want. You don't have to do any fancy breathing technique. Just allow yourself to breathe normally, but be aware of your breath: the total inhalation and the total exhalation.

Client: [*They close and open their eyes.*] I can't do it. I told you it wouldn't work.

Therapist: No problem. I thought it might be worth a try. Did you feel or hear anyone from the inside while you tried it?

Client: [*They pause.*] I just had a feeling I had to stop. I don't know where it came from, but it was strong.

Therapist: Would you be willing to check in to see if it was someone inside who was objecting to the conscious breathing?

Client: I'm not sure, but maybe it was Peter. He wants me to stay alert all the time.

Therapist: Are you in touch with him right now?

Client: He is nearby, yeah.

Therapist: Could you check in with him to see what his concerns might be? [*By addressing Peter, we are adding the second and third pillars into the discussion, which I will explore in chapters 5 and 6.*]

Client: [*They pause.*] He won't tell me his reasons.

Therapist: No problem. I'd like to try something different. For this one, you can leave your eyes open.

Client: Okay.

Therapist: I invite you to look around my office and tell me what you see. Before you do it, could you check in with Peter to see if he is okay with it?

Client: He says it's fine because he is always looking around anyway.

Therapist: Please tell him thanks for giving his permission.

Client: Okay.

Therapist: Please just look around. What do you see? Notice five or six things.

Client: I see your desk, a lamp, your bookcase, your laptop, the door, the window.

Therapist: Okay, listen carefully and tell me what you hear. See if you can come up with four things.

Client: I hear a shuffling sound out in the hallway. I heard your voice just a second ago. There. I hear a doorbell. Oh, I hear a ding from a cell phone somewhere far away.

Therapist: Excellent. Now use your hands to touch three things and describe them.

Client: I feel the softness of the arms of the chair. I feel the coarseness of my jeans. I feel the oiliness of my hair.

Therapist: Wonderful. Now notice any smells or tastes.

Client: I can just barely taste the mouthwash I used this morning. I can't smell anything.

Therapist: Okay, now tell me how anxious you are, what number on a scale of 0 to 10.

Client: A 4.

Therapist: I call what you just did "present timing." It is a mindfulness exercise. It is simply a way to be aware of your environment by going through each of your senses. It could also be called a grounding exercise.

Client: What do you mean by grounding?

Therapist: Let me walk you through an exercise to show you what grounding is. Is Peter still okay with this process?

Client: He isn't objecting.

Therapist: Okay. Try this. Wiggle your toes.

Client: Okay. It feels weird.

Therapist: Now, see if you can feel the bottom of your feet. [*In promoting body awareness, the bottoms of the feet are usually the easiest to become aware of.*]

Client: Yeah, sort of.

Therapist: Okay now without touching your ankles, I invite you to be aware of them.

Client: Okay.

Therapist: Now notice your legs. [*The therapist then continues with the hips, stomach, chest, arms, neck, face, and top of the head.*] What you just did is called grounding because it connects you to your body and, in a sense, to the ground below. Some people like to take their shoes off and walk in the grass or the dirt. That would be another way to feel grounded.

Client: I think I would feel silly doing that.

Therapist: It's not required, just an idea. Now let's finish by taking a big breath together. But before we do, please ask Peter if it's okay with him.

Client: He says it's fine as long as it is only one breath. [*They take a single deep breath.*]

Therapist: Great, and how was it for you?

Client: I guess I do feel a little better.

Therapist: Mindfulness is simply about being more aware of what is happening around you and what is happening within your own body.

Client: How will this help me?

Therapist: Do you remember when we talked about dissociation a couple weeks ago?

Client: Yeah.

Therapist: And how you ended up having some problems because of lost time?

Client: Yes.

Therapist: Well, mindfulness is the opposite of dissociation. It's a way to train yourself to stop dissociating so much. In future sessions, we can talk about other ways to practice mindfulness in your day-to-day life.

Client: I'm willing to try.

Depending on how willing the client is, there are many other mindfulness techniques that can be helpful in promoting increased body awareness, including yoga, progressive muscle relaxation, gardening, and forest bathing. If they are really committed, you might even suggest an eight-week mindfulness training system (Williams & Penman, 2011). They might also be interested in trying out emotional freedom techniques (EFT), thought field therapy (TFT), or self-hypnosis.

IMAGINATION

Some clients with DID are unwilling or unable to do any mindfulness or breathing exercises. Their reluctance might stem from skeptical internal alters, the fear of being too vulnerable, the emergence of uncomfortable emotions once they focus on the body, the release of physical pain, or some combination of these. When this happens, you can easily shift to a different method of resourcing: imagination.

Essentially, imaginative techniques allow the client to slightly dissociate from the body while constructing a mental image of something calm, relaxing, or centering. Once the client constructs a mental image, they are able to calm their body without experiencing the negative consequences of interoception. There are many possible techniques that can be utilized. For example, you can guide them to go inside their inner realm and find a safe building or room, or you can lead them in a guided meditation. Rather than expecting them to engage in interoception, you are providing them with enough distance from the body by engaging their thought processes instead. Rather than *feeling* sensations in their body, they can *think* about how various sensory experiences affect them.

Clients with DID generally have active imaginations, which is what made it possible for them to create alternate identities and rich inner worlds. The therapist can draw on these skills as a way to piggyback on other resourcing techniques. One effective method that draws on imagination is a guided meditation, as illustrated in the following dialogue:

Therapist: I have another idea for a way for you to practice calming yourself down without any kind of breathing. It involves the imagination. Would you be willing to try it today?

Client: I guess so.

Therapist: Good. Can you think of a time when you were somewhere in nature and felt calm, relaxed, or centered? [*It is best to avoid the word* safe, *as some clients have never felt safe, but they may be able to remember a time when they felt calm or centered.*]

Client: [*They pause.*] There was a time when I went fishing with my grandpa. It was by a creek. I was pretty little.

Therapist: Excellent. I invite you to close your eyes and imagine being by the creek right now.

Client: Okay. [*They close their eyes.*] I can sort of see the creek, but it is pretty vague.

Therapist: That's fine. Can you describe it?

Client: I think it's the same creek where my grandpa and I used to go fishing. There are trees nearby.

Therapist: What season is it?

Client: Summer.

Therapist: How far away is the creek now?

Client: I'm walking on a path toward it now.

Therapist: Excellent. Take your time and when you are ready, see if you can describe what you see in more detail.

Client: [*They begin again after a long silence.*] I can see sticks floating down the creek. There is a slight breeze.

Therapist: What else do you see?

Client: The sky is clear, hardly any clouds.

Therapist: Where are you now?

Client: I am near the water. There is a log. I'm going to sit on it. [*At this point, the therapist asks the client to describe their experience, activating each of the client's senses. Once that is complete, the conversation continues.*]

Therapist: While you sit on the log, would it be possible for you to focus on your breath?

Client: Okay, yeah. The air so clean and refreshing. [*In this example, the client is able to do some conscious breathing while in this imaginary calm place, which they weren't able to do previously while sitting in the therapist's office.*]

Therapist: Before you come back, I would like you to take one last look around and experience this place fully.

Client: Okay.

Therapist: Now I would invite you to think of one word or phrase that describes this place so you can easily remember how to get back here on your own.

Client: Brook.

Therapist: Excellent. Now I would invite you to take the word *brook* and place it somewhere in this imaginary place: in the sky, on the ground, by a tree, wherever you wish.

Client: I put it in the creek.

Therapist: Perfect. Now please look carefully at the word *brook*. Can you see the letters?

Client: Yes, they are just floating there.

Therapist: What color are they?

Client: White with red borders.

Therapist: Okay, I invite you to look at the word one more time. Remember in the future, if you ever want to return to this space, all you have to do is recall this word, and remember its white coloring and red borders.

Client: Okay, I've got it.

Therapist: Now take a couple breaths, open your eyes, and return your attention to this room.

Client: [*They open their eyes.*]

Therapist: How do you feel right now?

Client: Pretty calm actually.

Before ending the session, the therapist in this example would do well to remind the client of their ability to return to this imaginary calm place any time they wish by closing their eyes and imaging the word *brook* with its white coloring and red border. The therapist can even invite the client to try it out quickly and see if it works. In future sessions, the therapist can use this resourcing tool with the client as needed.

As with any guided resourcing technique, it is important that you maintain a strong attunement with the client. In order to do so, you must stay alert to the client's facial expressions and body language. At the same time, you must remain resourced within yourself, using conscious breathing or other methods that work well. The concentration required can be arduous, as you must be able to remain focused during long silences. Knowing when to remain silent and when to intervene with a simple question like "What's happening now?" is difficult. If the attunement between you and client is strong, then subtle cues, sometimes just beneath conscious awareness, will guide you in this regard. Since it is not necessary to get it right all the time, aspiration 7 will hopefully suffice: "Trust the process rather than focusing on your expectations for the outcome."

CHAPTER 5

GETTING TO KNOW THE ALTERS: THE SECOND PILLAR

By definition, clients who meet criteria for DID experience identity disruptions marked by the presence of two or more personality states (APA, 2022). Another way to say this is that a client with DID is a system of alters, all contained within one body. It can be tempting to set up templates regarding the types and roles of alters in a DID system—for example, the designation of "emotional parts" and "apparently normal parts" as with structural dissociation theory, or the designation of "managers, firefighters, and exiles" as with IFS—given that this provides you with an organized way of thinking about parts. I agree that such designations are often helpful in working with clients who do not have DID, but not for clients with DID. If you want to respect and honor the variety and complexity of the client's inner world, the creative ways in which alters are organized, and each individual alter's ability to adopt and change roles, any preconceived ideas are likely to be counterproductive.

It is more important for the client's system to learn about itself than for you to get to know each alter, though whenever you do learn new information about particular alters, it enhances the therapeutic process. There are many possible reasons for this enhancement. First, when a client brings up a problem in therapy, it is important to understand that the alter who brings up the problem is not the only participant in that problem. There will almost certainly be other alters involved. The more information that you have about the other alters, the more helpful you can be in helping the client address that problem.

Second, as mentioned in chapter 4, attunement is an essential form of resourcing. The trust that the primary alter has in you goes far in moving the therapy along in an effective manner. However, even strong attunement with the primary alter can falter quickly if other alters are reluctant or hostile toward the therapeutic process. By getting to know these other alters, and establishing communication and understanding with them, agreements can sometimes be made to bring them on board or at least get them to agree to stand aside and not interfere with the therapeutic process.

Third, one of the most disruptive symptoms that many clients with DID experience is losing blocks of time with significant amnesia. The more alters you get to know, the more likely you will be able to assist the client in discovering who was fronting the body during those experiences. This, in turn, can assist the client in improving awareness or creating more co-consciousness so they can fill those gaps, eventually reducing or eliminating them all together.

In this chapter, I discuss the process of getting to know the alters, which is characterized by three steps: (1) being introduced to the alters, (2) learning more about their roles, and (3) getting curious about their internal world.

INTRODUCTIONS OF ALTERS

Once you have confirmed a diagnosis of DID, and both you and the client are accepting of it, you might suggest the possibility of getting introduced to any alters who may wish to meet you. You can explain that this will give the alters a chance to be seen and accepted, as well as an opportunity to share any concerns or ideas they have for therapy. However, you need to step away from any expectation that all the alters will agree to come forward and be interviewed. First, there will likely be some alters who will never agree to take over the client's body, even for a few minutes, in order to meet you. They will have their own reasons for their reticence. Perhaps they remember being abused the last time they inhabited the body. Perhaps they are frightened of the intense sensory input that occurs when doing so. Maybe they are just too shy to do so. Second, there may be alters who are hidden away, concealed from even the primary. Third, there may be alters who are so full of anger and aggression that it wouldn't be safe for them to take over the body.

If the client agrees to proceed with introducing certain alters to you, it is important to consider the switching process. A switch in identities occurs whenever one alter "steps back" from fronting the body and a different alter "steps forward" to take over the responsibility of fronting the body. With some client systems, this process is highly structured. There may be curtains, doors, or portals that alters must pass through to make a switch. In other systems, it "just happens," and few, if any, of the alters are aware of the occurrence. Despite media portrayals of characters undergoing dramatic changes in affect and appearance when switching identities, most clients with DID have learned how to undertake such a transition without anyone noticing, except perhaps the most informed and acutely aware observer.

If a client has been in therapy for a reasonable length of time, it is highly likely that some switching of alters has already occurred during therapy sessions. In my experience, it is common to meet an alter for what I thought was the first time, only for the alter to inform me that we had talked previously during a session.

Even though most clients with DID have already had numerous experiences of switching identities, there is a great deal of variability as to their awareness or control of the process. Switching can occur spontaneously when a client is triggered by an event in their environment, or when something shifts in their inner world. Some clients experience a headache after a switch, especially when the switch takes place precipitously. For these and other reasons, it can be helpful for you to tentatively offer some assistance. One simple method to assist in the switching process is described in the following dialogue:

Therapist: Thank you for allowing me to meet some of the other alters in your system. I know you already know how to initiate a switch, but I was wondering if you would be willing to allow me to help you slow down the process a little.

Jordan: [*Jordan is the primary alter.*] That would be alright.

Therapist: Okay, who is first in line for me to meet?

Jordan: It's a little boy.

Therapist: What's his name?

Jordan: Georgie.

Therapist: How old is he?

Jordan: Six.

Therapist: Can you sense him right now?

Jordan: Yeah, he is strong. He's eager to take over.

Therapist: I am going to count from one to five. With each number I say, you will back off a little and Georgie will move forward a little. Okay?

Jordan: Yeah.

Therapist: When I get to the number three, you two will pass each other. When I get to five, you—Jordan—will be inside and Georgie will be fronting the body.

Jordan: You better start soon because he is pushing.

Therapist: Okay. One. You are moving back and Georgie is moving forward. Two. [*The therapist takes a short pause.*] Three. You are passing each other. Four. Georgie is getting closer. Five. Hi there.

Georgie: [*He looks around the office, then looks down.*]

Therapist: Georgie? [*Georgie nods his head slightly.*] Thanks for coming out to meet me.

At this point in the conversation, the therapist notices that Georgie is either shy or scared. Since Georgie is only six years old, the therapist should offer him a toy, drawing paper, or whatever other materials they usually provide to child clients. After interacting for a while, the therapist can use the same procedure, except in this case counting backward from five to one to either bring Jordan back or allow the next alter in line to come out. At some point, it would also be helpful to ask the various alters what the switching process was like for them and if they were able to see the other alter when they passed each other on number three.

It is important to consult with each alter regarding their experience of the switching process to determine whether to continue with this method or use another. One key element of this method is that it encourages the alters involved to be conscious of the process. Hopefully, this will lead to a reduction of amnesia and loss of time. Sometimes after a few times, the client will indicate that the slow process of switching is no longer necessary because they have figured out their own method of conscious switching.

Types of Alters

As I have indicated earlier, it is a mistake to set up arbitrary categories or structures from which to define a client's system, as every system will be different. There are, however, certain types of alters who appear within many systems, and it can be helpful to be aware of these as long as you don't hold on to the mindset that every system must have these particular types of alters.

Primary

The primary is simply the alter who is most often in charge of fronting the body and dealing with the outside world. In some systems, this role is obvious, and the primary is a responsible adult who is mostly in charge. In other cases, this is not always clear. Some systems are not well-organized, and there may be several alters who come and go, taking on the responsibilities of the primary in a way that may appear random to you. In these cases, one of your first goals is to help the system clarify, elevate, or designate one or more alters to take on the role of a responsible adult. (In working with children or adolescents, it may make more sense to consider which alter is the "most responsible.")

Responsible Adults

The responsible adult (or adults) is the decision maker for all actions the client takes in the outside world. When a client system has a strong primary, it is usually safe to assume that the primary is serving as the responsible adult. However, this is not always the case. Sometimes the primary will appear passive and may have amnesia to many behaviors and activities that result in unfavorable consequences. Actions have consequences, so I make it a priority to let clients know that despite their diagnosis, and regardless of any amnesia they may experience or which alter is fronting the body at the time, they must accept the consequences of their actions in the outside world. As their therapist, I am unwilling to defend or excuse them for any of those actions.

In my experience, almost all clients readily accept this position as obvious, partly because they tend to go overboard in blaming themselves even for things that are not their fault. There are certainly situations where a client might fabricate or exaggerate their symptoms to avoid criminal or civil penalties for their actions, but ideally, you will have already identified these individuals as malingering in your initial assessments and have ruled out a diagnosis of DID. If not, clients who try to persuade you that they should be excused from such consequences will raise red flags for you regarding their diagnosis. I must clarify here, however, that there may indeed be individual alters who are quick to pass the responsibility onto other alters. This in itself is not problematic as long as the client understands that the whole system must bear the consequences of actions taken by any alter in that system.

By taking a strong position in this regard, you underscore the importance of one or more alters stepping up to serve as responsible adults. Once they accept this responsibility, it behooves them to pay closer attention to which alters have the ability and interest in fronting the body, and it increases their motivation to exert some control over that process. While you want to encourage those responsible adults to exercise such control, you are also responsible for encouraging them to communicate and cooperate (the third pillar—the three Cs) with those alters who are prone to fronting the body and doing destructive things, such as using alcohol or drugs, self-harming, or engaging in other dangerous behaviors. You will need to help them understand that exerting control without demonstrating empathy or nurturing these alters will be unlikely to be successful in the long run.

Another role of the responsible adult or adults is to take responsibility for the child alters in the system. Just as it would be considered child neglect to allow children to run amuck without any supervision or nurturance in the outside world, the same is true within the inner world of a client with DID. What this means specifically is that young alters need responsible alters inside who take on the role of watching over them and not leaving them alone. The following dialogue illustrates how you might approach this issue with a client:

Therapist: I would like to talk a little more about your suspicion that someone else drove your car, if that's okay with you.

Tracy: [*Tracy is the primary alter.*] I checked the odometer this morning, and someone drove my car for over eighteen miles between last night, when I put it in the garage, and this morning, when I drove here to my appointment.

Therapist: Do you have any theories as to who that could have been?

Tracy: I have to admit it makes no sense that someone broke into my garage, drove my car for eighteen miles, and then returned it to the garage.

Therapist: That does seem unlikely, unless you have given a copy of your key to someone?

Tracy: You know me well enough that I would never do that.

Therapist: So, what does that leave?

Tracy: Either I drove it and forgot, or someone inside did it without my knowledge.

Therapist: Did you find any other evidence of what might have happened? New purchases? Your car keys in a different place? Things like that?

Tracy: The car keys were on the hook by the front door where I always leave them. Come to think of it, there were candy wrappers on the bedroom floor, and I don't usually eat candy in bed.

Therapist: Is there anyone inside who is fond of that particular brand of candy?

Tracy: Only Renee, but she's only ten years old. I don't think she would be able to drive the car.

Therapist: Is there anyone else inside who might have been helping her with a project like that?

Renee: [*She stirs.*] You're asking too many questions.

Therapist: Hi there, who am I talking to? [*The therapist pauses.*] Renee?

Renee: Just leave it alone. Nothing bad happened.

Therapist: Thanks for being part of this conversation, Renee. I'm wondering if Tracy is nearby and can listen in.

Renee: She's too bossy. Sometimes I just need to do things myself.

Therapist: Tracy says you're ten years old. Is that true?

Renee: I didn't drive the car, if that's what you're thinking.

Therapist: Oh, I'm glad to hear that. Driving can be dangerous if you aren't old enough.

Renee: I'm not telling you who helped me. I've got to go now.

Tracy: I'm back.

Therapist: Tracy?

Tracy: Yeah, it's me.

Therapist: Did you hear my conversation with Renee?

Tracy: Most of it. She's a little shit.

Therapist: Do you have any idea who might have helped her?

Tracy: No, but I'll find out tonight when we have our internal family meeting.

Therapist: That sounds good. I know you have stepped up to be the responsible adult for your system, and I know it's a challenge.

Tracy: That's for sure. I told you, she's a handful. I don't know how to control her.

Therapist: Did you hear her say that she needs to do things by herself sometimes?

Tracy: No, I must have missed that.

Therapist: Are you able to talk to her right now?

Tracy: I can try. [*She closes her eyes in silence.*]

Therapist: What is she saying?

Tracy: She's acting all mad and upset.

Therapist: I'm wondering if you could find out from her what she needs from you. Maybe if you helped her to feel better, she wouldn't feel like she had to break your rules.

Tracy: I just heard from Carey. He admitted to driving. He said he didn't want to, but he only did it so Renee wouldn't.

Therapist: Isn't Carey the alter who you said might be able to help you with your adult responsibilities?

Tracy: Yeah, but that sure didn't work out, did it?

Therapist: Do you know if Carey tried to get in touch with you before driving the car?

Tracy: [*She pauses.*] He says he did, but I don't remember that happening.

Therapist: Our time is about up. Is it possible that you and Carey still might be able to work together to prevent the little ones from taking over? Tell me what you think about this, but I wonder if Renee, and possibly the other little ones, need more attention and supervision from you and Carey.

Tracy: Maybe. I like to yell at them, but Carey seems to be nicer to them.

Therapist: I don't know if it would work, but I do know that ten-year-olds not only need supervision but also lots of love and support.

Tracy: I'm not so good at the love part.

Therapist: Could Carey help you with that?

Tracy: I don't know. To tell you the truth, I doubt it.

Therapist: Well, I encourage you to keep the lines of communication open with Carey and Renee, and let me know next week what you've come up with.

In this scenario, the therapist was able to emphasize how important the role of the responsible adult could be for the client, by incorporating both pillar two (getting to know the alters) and parts of pillar three (inner communication and cooperation, which you will learn about in the next chapter). In addition, it placed the responsibility back on the client to find new ways of effectively solving the problem posed by Tracy at the beginning of the session: someone driving her car.

Protectors

It is common for clients with DID to have one or more alters who can correctly be described as *protectors*. They can be any age and are often angry. Sometimes, they direct their anger outward, even having fantasies of invoking revenge against the people who abused and traumatized them in the past. Other times, they tend to direct their anger at other alters in the system. Either way, it is important for you to understand the motivations that underlie their emotions, attitudes, and actions.

For example, a system may have a protective alter who verbally abuses a child alter, acting similarly to a past perpetrator. As you and others in the system get to know this protector, you may discover that the alter is trying to toughen up the child to protect them from more serious abuse. Alternatively, the protector may be calling the child derogatory names to keep them from taking over the body and doing something dangerous.

Another possibility is that the protector either witnessed or experienced a trauma when the client was a child, and the perpetrator of that trauma threatened harm to the client—or someone the client cared for—if the child told anyone what happened. Even though the client is now grown up and safe from such threats, the protector alter doesn't fully understand that and will do almost anything to prevent the primary from revealing the memory of the abuse. If the protector can be convinced of the new reality—perhaps the perpetrator is deceased or the client has moved far away and is clearly safe—they may back off from their opposition. In the best-case scenario, the protector might be willing to discover a new way to defend the primary alter that is actually helpful. For example, the protector may remind the primary of the next appointment time or stay nearby during therapy to make sure the primary doesn't share too much too quickly.

Adolescents

Most client systems have one or more adolescent alters, who were likely created to handle certain traumatic experiences that occurred in adolescence. As you might suspect, these alters often express ambivalence with regard to questions or positions. Just like adolescents in the outside world, these alters tend to distrust adults because, on the one hand, they want to be independent, but on the other hand, they want to continue to be supported, helped, and acknowledged. For this reason, therapists who are effective in working with actual adolescent clients would do well to utilize those same skills when working with an adolescent alter.

By encouraging the responsible adults in the client system to trust the adolescents with certain responsibilities, such as watching over the little ones, the adolescents are more likely to feel respected. At the same time, you want the system to provide opportunities for the adolescent to take over the body and make time for fun, such as playing video games or listening to music, as this makes the adolescent more likely to become an ally and a productive member of the system, and less likely to get into trouble.

One thing to watch out for when working with adolescent alters is their tendency to get involved in risky behaviors, which is a good reason to form an alliance with them early in the therapy process, with the hope of reducing this behavior in the future. If the primary recounts some of these risky behaviors during an initial assessment and you are not aware of the client's multiplicity at the time, you might misinterpret those experiences as manic or hypomanic episodes when in fact they were the unsupervised behavior of an adolescent alter.

Children

As you will learn in chapter 7, the identity fragmentation that occurs in DID dates back to childhood, so clients with this condition will almost always have one or more child alters of different ages. Some are preverbal, others are toddlers, and others are school age. It is valuable for you to think of these alters similarly to children in a family, and part of the therapeutic work will involve providing psychoeducation to help your client understand this.

For example, in a family, it is not acceptable to leave a baby, toddler, or young child alone for even a short amount of time. Rather, an adolescent or adult must provide supervision at all times. This is also true inside a client system. Unless you point this out, the client may not have thought about it. Instead, they may have inner children who run amok inside their internal world or who spend all day hidden in a closet or crying under a bed. These little ones may also take over the body at will and create problems in the client's social life.

It can be difficult working with a client when their child alters are not adequately supervised or supported. One reason for this is that adult and adolescent alters often have strong animosity or even hatred toward those child alters. They may do their best to ignore these little ones, verbally abuse them, or wish they would disappear or go away. In this situation, it can be helpful to have conversations with the client about their values and principles regarding how children should be treated. While most responsible adult alters in DID systems are strongly against child abuse in the real world, it may not have occurred to them that by neglecting or abusing their internal children, they are perpetuating the same treatment they are so vehemently against. When you gently point this out, the client is often able to change their attitudes and behaviors toward those internal children.

If the client is a parent, it can also be helpful to elicit their beliefs about child-rearing. Many will describe feelings of guilt on the occasions when they stepped away from their best judgment by yelling at their child. Once the client shares with you their values and principles regarding child-rearing, you can ask them whether they are able to apply these principles to their relationships with the little ones inside. This can involve discussing which alters might be willing to adopt a child-rearing or babysitting role toward the child alters.

It can be challenging, however, to provide this input to a client without activating their sense of failure. One way to circumvent this is to take a deep dive into their values and principles more generally, which may include a strong commitment to justice, a belief in the importance of taking care of the children, or a desire to end the cycle of abuse that has been going on for generations in their family of origin. It may be helpful to ask how, in spite of the power of such a cycle, your client was able to challenge the norm and develop different values. How have they been able to hold on to those values for so long given the trauma they have experienced? All of us fall short at times in staying true to our values, but that doesn't discount the values altogether. In fact, when we realize that we have fallen short, it can amplify our commitment to those values.

Other Types of Alters

As mentioned previously, clients with DID tend to be highly creative, so they can have unusual alters such as animals, spiritual or otherworldly beings, demons, or inanimate objects. The *DSM-5-TR* notes that the experience of being possessed by demons or other spirits is broadly accepted in some cultural and religious practices, in which case a client would not meet the criteria for DID. However, if these experiences of possession are disconnected from such cultural or religious practices, are unwanted and involuntary, and cause significant distress, this may indicate a DID diagnosis referred to as possession-form dissociative identity disorder (APA, 2022).

It is important to emphasize, however, that the *DSM*'s acceptance of these symptoms as indicative of DID does not mean that the *DSM* subscribes to the idea that these clients are actually possessed by entities from outside themselves, which might require some sort of exorcism ritual to treat. Rather, it acknowledges that cultural influences are important in determining the manner in which alters are formed and sustained, as well as the roles they may adopt in a particular system.

All alters deserve acknowledgment and respect, with the overwhelming assumption that they are serving the system in some way, even if the alter's actions are initially harmful to the system. There are times when other alters in the system have to hold back a dangerous alter and not allow it to take over the body, but the long-term goal is always to find a way to reeducate the dangerous alter so it understands that there are better ways to serve the system.

ROLES

One way to acknowledge and authenticate an alter is to be curious about the role or roles they play in the system. Since conflicts among alters is common, the idea that alters could be playing a role in the system may be difficult for clients to understand or agree with. When there are angry and disruptive alters present, they are often perceived by the other alters as enemies to be outcast or eliminated. Clearly, however, those alters were created by the system for a reason—in particular, to assist the client in surviving. It is almost certainly true that the role they played years ago when the client was being traumatized is no longer functional or helpful to the system in the present, but the alter may not be aware of this because they are stuck in the past, often reliving the trauma inside the inner world. This is where reeducation can be enormously helpful.

The following dialogue is an example of how you might explore roles with a client and help them subscribe to the idea that whatever role a particular alter is playing, it is ultimately in service of the system:

Therapist: I remember the last time we met, you spoke about an alter named Conner who has been creating some chaos in your life. You indicated you would check with him in between sessions to see if he would be willing to meet with me.

Amy: [*Amy is the primary alter.*] I remember.

Therapist: Were you able to have that conversation?

Amy: Sort of. He didn't answer me in words, but I feel his presence right now and he wants to come out.

Therapist: Do you think it would be safe to let him front the body right now?

Amy: I think so. He's been less active this week.

Therapist: I'd like to set some ground rules before he comes out, if that would be okay with you.

Amy: Whatever you think.

Therapist: I just want to make sure it's safe.

Amy: Okay. What did you have in mind?

Therapist: I'd like to see if you could get a commitment from Conner on a couple things.

Amy: I'll try.

Therapist: I'd like Conner to agree to not leave the room and to not resort to violence. He also needs to agree to go back inside before the end of the session to let you come out.

Amy: [*She pauses.*] He agrees.

Therapist: Please let him know that he is not required to answer any of my questions, and he can go back inside anytime.

Amy: Okay. He's ready.

Therapist: Would you like me to work with you so he can come out slowly, like we did once before?

Conner: No need, I'm already here.

Therapist: Oh, I'm happy to meet you. Do you know who I am?

Conner: Of course, what do you want? I don't have all day.

Therapist: Were you listening in to my conversation with Amy?

Conner: What do you think? I know everything Amy does. Most of it I don't approve of.

Therapist: Amy tells me she got into trouble at work because you came out and criticized her boss.

Conner: Yeah, she deserved it. Amy is too passive. She lets her boss run over her all the time. I had to do something.

Therapist: I see. Are you saying you were trying to stand up for her?

Conner: If she can't grow a backbone, I have to provide one for her.

Therapist: I was wondering if Amy is close by and able to hear this, as she might not have understood why you did that.

Conner: Oh, she understands alright. She's worried she'll get fired.

Therapist: I'm so glad you realize that.

Conner: I wish she would quit. There are other jobs. Amy doesn't deserve to be treated badly. We've had too much of that in our life.

Therapist: Have you tried to protect her from harm in the past as well?

Conner: It was harder then. I don't want to talk about it. Are you done with all your questions? I have things to do.

Although connecting Conner's role in the past as a protector with his present role could be helpful to the system, the timing of the question was too soon, so the therapist attempts to rectify the mistake as they continue the conversation.

Therapist: Remember our agreement. You can leave anytime, but I do want to apologize for my question, as now I see it wasn't a very good question.

Conner: Okay. So, what else do you want to know?

Therapist: I wonder if you'd be willing to have a talk with Amy so she understands your motivation for what you did.

Conner: I shouldn't have to explain everything to her. She should already know these things.

Therapist: I understand what you are saying.

Conner: Do you, really? She listens to you. Just tell her to be more aggressive. Then I won't have to. Anyway, I've got to go.

Therapist: Okay, thanks for coming out and talking to me.

Amy: He's already gone. I'm back.

Therapist: Can you let him know I appreciate the opportunity to talk to him.

Amy: He hears you.

Therapist: Good. Were you able to hear my conversation with him?

Amy: Most of it. He may mean well, but he doesn't understand how this is the best job I've had in years, and if I left, I'd have a hard time getting anything better. In fact, I'd probably have to take a pay cut. [*She begins to tear up.*] Now he's mocking me for crying. I can't stand him!

Therapist: I can see you're hurting right now. Take your time.

Amy: [*She pauses as she grabs a tissue.*] Can't you just tell him to lay off? What he's doing is making it worse.

Therapist: I'm wondering if you've thought about how your anger at Conner may be affecting him? [*Amy is silent.*] Could it be that he needs some acknowledgment from you that he is trying his best to protect you, even if he is perhaps coming on too strong?

Amy: I never thought about it that way.

At this point, the therapist makes a guess that the relationship with Amy is strong enough that she would be able to tolerate this conversation, and if not, that she would be able to let the therapist know.

Therapist: I brought up the past with him, and he told me he wasn't ready to talk about it. That is totally okay by me. In fact, I think it was too early for me to even bring it up with him. Would that be true for you too?

Amy: Maybe. I'm not sure.

Therapist: Well, I wonder if you've thought about whether Conner was around when you were little and life was a lot harder.

Amy: I'm sure he was.

Therapist: Do you have a sense of what his role was back then?

Amy: He tried to fight my battles, but it was hopeless.

Therapist: I'm not asking you to go back to those memories right now. What I'm wondering about is whether Conner fully understands that you have more options and are safer now as an adult than you were as a child.

Amy: Why wouldn't he understand?

Therapist: I'm not sure, but sometimes alters get stuck in the past. Is he listening now?

Amy: No, he went off to his little cottage.

Therapist: Maybe you can think about it between now and our next session, and if you feel up to it, try to talk to him in the interim.

Amy: I will try.

Therapist: I'm glad these issues are coming out in the open. As we've talked about in the past, these are conflicts that you and Conner need to work out together. I'm happy to offer as much assistance and support as I can, but it is going to be up to you two to find a compromise or some other kind of solution. Does that make sense to you?

Amy: It makes sense, but I don't particularly like it.

This dialogue exemplifies several aspirations: "Remind yourself that your client is the whole system, not any particular alter" (aspiration 2), "Center the client system in therapy rather than yourself as the expert" (aspiration 3), and "Foster an abundance of curiosity regarding the client's system" (aspiration 4). Toward the end of the conversation, the therapist and client have just begun to touch on the issue of roles. Future conversations might revolve around understanding what role Conner played when the system was a child versus the role he is playing now. Questions to consider include: What would help Amy understand Conner's intentions rather than get upset with the result of his behavior? How could Amy help Conner understand how different life is now for her than when they were little? If they could both realize that Conner is trying his best to protect her, could she explain to him a better way to protect her? If the client can answer these questions and understand why they are important, it opens the door to Conner becoming an ally for Amy rather than continuing to cause problems in her life.

INTERNAL WORLDS

It is vitally important to familiarize yourself with the details and structures of a client's internal world when working with DID. Unless you express curiosity and ask questions about this world, you may miss rich opportunities to learn more about the client's life, and along with it, an abundance of therapeutic opportunities for healing. Your first task is to suspend disbelief about this inner realm because, to the alters in the system, the inner world is as real, and sometimes more real, than the outside world. Aspiration 6 becomes relevant in this regard: "Have the courage to enter the client's inner realm while always staying grounded in this realm."

I like to think of these internal worlds as *paracosms*, or detailed imaginary worlds originating in childhood. Some successful writers, including Robert Louis Stevenson, J. R. R Tolkien, and C. S. Lewis, have recounted childhood paracosms as influencing their writing. In addition, up to 17 percent of children reported having created paracosms that they are able to describe in great detail (Taylor et al., 2015, 2020). These creations peak at the age of nine and are less common after the age of twelve, and they are more common among highly creative children.

There are many other accounts of imaginary worlds as well. Examples include the Sufi creation story, where God used a tiny leftover piece of clay the size of a sesame seed to create an alternative "in-between Earth," a world of the imagination (Nooney, 2022). Other examples include the Jungian personal or collective unconscious, and the dreamscape we all visit at night.

The paracosms created by clients with DID often have complex inner landscapes inhabited by their alters. The complexity and variety of these internal worlds cannot be understated. They can be confined to small spaces or encompass large fields with rivers, mountain ranges, caves, and underground passageways. They can contain buildings and other structures, rooms with video projections of the outside world, human-sized board games, or cloud platforms designed as gathering places. There may also be play areas, secret rooms, hidden alcoves, or hiding spaces. The alters can change the landscape for their own needs and purposes, establish communication with one another, endure conflicts, and share memories, sometimes without the knowledge of the primary alter who is running the body and keeping track of day-to-day needs and relationships.

As the various alters of the client's system begin to trust you, they may share details about their internal world. In doing so, they will also provide important information about the alters living there. Another way to think about these paracosms is with the metaphor of the rabbit hole.* By seizing upon a genuine curiosity about the client's inner world, you are able to step one foot into the rabbit hole, while keeping the other foot resourced in the material world. Note again aspiration 6: "Have the courage to enter your client's inner realm while always staying grounded in this realm."

---

* The titular character in Lewis Carroll's 1865 novel *Alice in Wonderland* falls down a rabbit hole to a dreamlike world of the imagination, which could also be described as a paracosm (Nooney, 2022).

Due to the creative diversity of clients with DID, it is important to not have any preconceived notions as to how these inner worlds "should" be structured. If you entertain any of these beliefs—whether it is a belief about the kinds of alters and their roles that "should" or "ought to" be present, or a belief that a certain kind of hierarchy *must* be involved—this will very likely be negatively perceived by at least some of the alters. If the client wishes to please you, they may even try to reinterpret their internal system in an attempt to mold their own experience to match your view, which would be disempowering and countertherapeutic.

Even while embracing aspiration 3—"Center the client system in therapy rather than yourself as the expert"—you may wish for some way to conceptualize the descriptions your clients share with you about their systems. For this reason, I have put together both a dimensional and a categorical model for your consideration.

The dimensional model places the ten attributes of a client's system on a scale from 1 to 10, with higher numbers indicating higher functioning. The first six attributes refer to the inner world of the client: its complexity, its structure, how well it is organized, the number of levels or layers of alters, how well-defined the responsible adults are, and how rigid the dissociative barriers are between the alters. By rating these six attributes, a picture begins to form as to the unique characteristics of your client's inner world.

The next four scales rate how well the client system has mastered the third pillar (communication, cooperation, and co-consciousness [the three Cs]) and how effective the system is in supervising and nurturing the child alters. These four scales provide a tentative assessment of the client's internal stability (see figure 2).

Figure 2: Dimensional Model

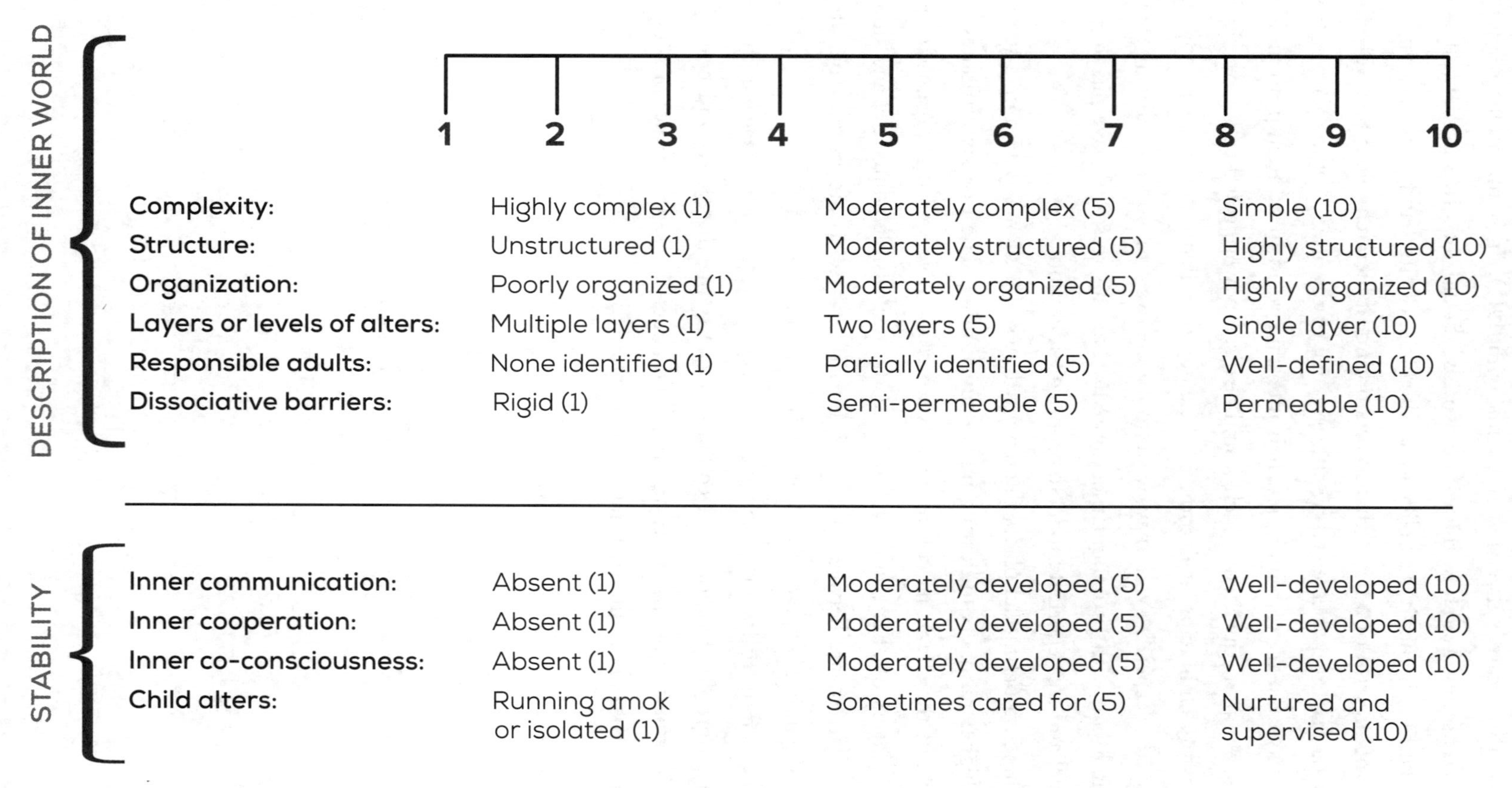

By rating all ten attributes early in the therapy process, you can create a tentative baseline of client system strengths, as well as areas for improvement. If desired, you can assess the client at different points in the therapy process as a way to note changes, including where there has been improvement and where there is more work to do. It is also possible to simply add the score for each attribute and divide by 10, which will give you the average score. You can then compare the client's average score at different points in the therapy process, aiming for higher scores overall. You can also separate the first six attributes from the last four and calculate the average score for each of these subsections. Generally, progress will be quicker in the last four attributes, as the child alters are taken better care of and the client begins to master the three Cs. Hopefully, these changes will also result in improvements in the first six attributes as the client's system begins to shift into a healthier organizational structure.

In addition to using the dimensional model to conceptualize client systems, you can also use a categorical model, which is a continuum that provides examples of how these attributes might coalesce into types of dissociative systems. It is important to note that these categories are fluid and changeable, which is why the border lines for each category are dotted lines rather than solid lines (see figure 3). In addition, I purposely did not include a scale on the dimensional model indicating the number of alters in the system because, in my view, the number of levels or layers of alters is more important than the total number. However, in the categorical model, I have offered a tentative number of alters that are likely to exist in the top layer of some of the categories.

Figure 3: Categorical Model

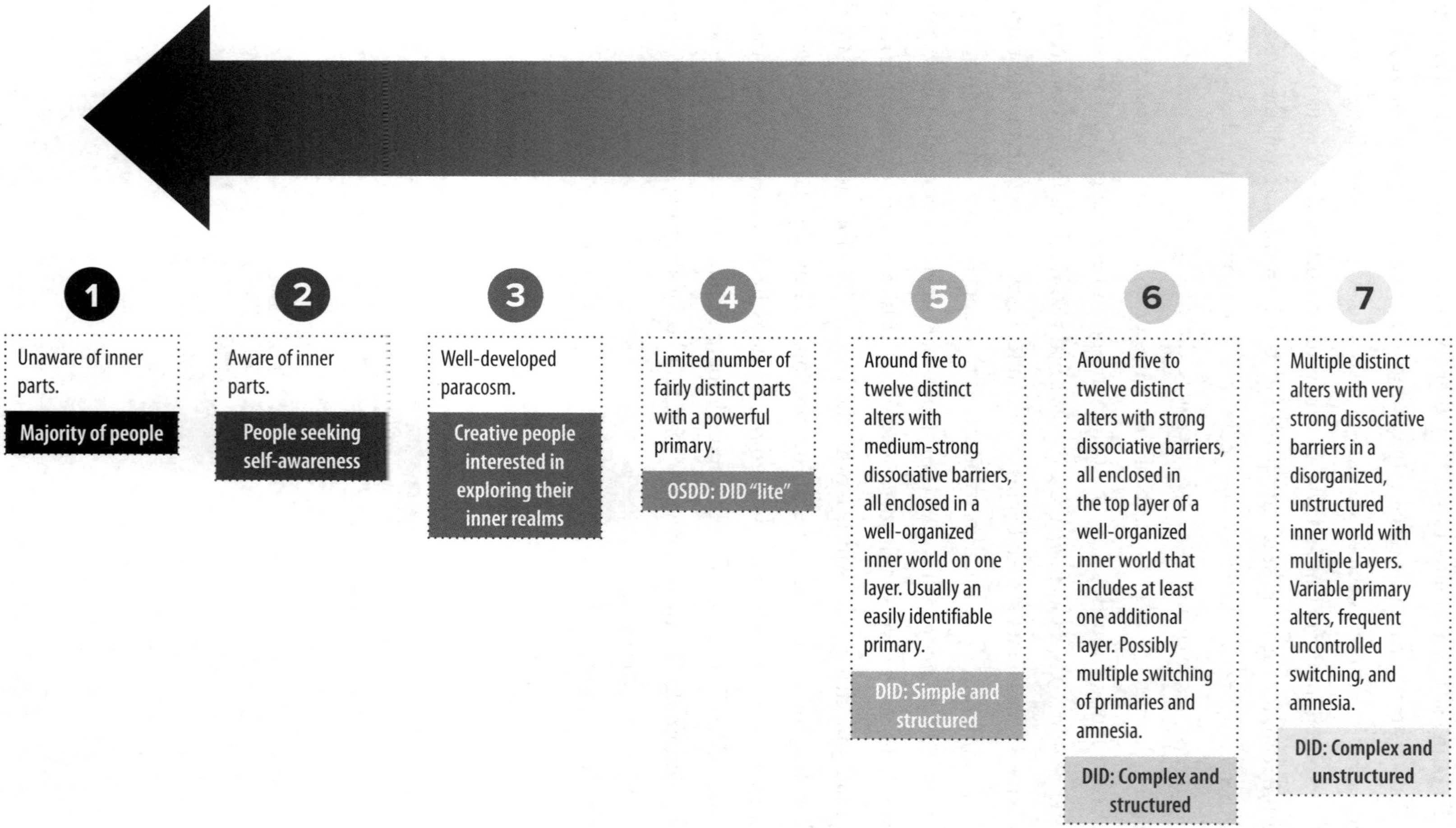

1	2	3	4	5	6	7
Unaware of inner parts.	Aware of inner parts.	Well-developed paracosm.	Limited number of fairly distinct parts with a powerful primary.	Around five to twelve distinct alters with medium-strong dissociative barriers, all enclosed in a well-organized inner world on one layer. Usually an easily identifiable primary.	Around five to twelve distinct alters with strong dissociative barriers, all enclosed in the top layer of a well-organized inner world that includes at least one additional layer. Possibly multiple switching of primaries and amnesia.	Multiple distinct alters with very strong dissociative barriers in a disorganized, unstructured inner world with multiple layers. Variable primary alters, frequent uncontrolled switching, and amnesia.
Majority of people	**People seeking self-awareness**	**Creative people interested in exploring their inner realms**	**OSDD: DID "lite"**	**DID: Simple and structured**	**DID: Complex and structured**	**DID: Complex and unstructured**

The first three categories are of people whose multiplicity, or lack thereof, would generally not be diagnosed as problematic. The first category describes the majority of people who are unaware of their inner parts.* The second category includes those who are interested in their inner parts as a way to improve their self-awareness. The third category are those who are in the process of extensively pursuing their inner worlds and have constructed elaborate paracosms.

The next four categories on the continuum are those who can be reasonably diagnosed with a dissociative disorder. The fourth category could best be described as a client diagnosed with OSDD. On the dimensional scales (see figure 2), they will generally rate as low complexity, highly structured and organized, and having permeable or semi-permeable dissociative barriers. They will have a well-defined responsible adult or adults, and there will be only one layer or level within the internal system. The alters are less likely to front the body than for those with a full-blown DID diagnosis, and when they do, amnesia is often absent because the primary is more likely to experience co-consciousness.

The fifth through seventh categories on the categorical model are clients who meet criteria for a diagnosis of DID. Client systems that fall into the *simple and structured* category generally rate as low complexity, highly structured, moderately to highly organized, and having semi-permeable dissociative barriers between alters, all on one level. These systems most often have a primary serving as a well-defined responsible adult. It may be difficult to distinguish this diagnosis from those with OSDD, as the dimensional ratings may be similar. One common difference is that those with OSDD tend to have alters fronting the body less often, and when they do, the system is more likely to have a primary who can remain co-conscious, resulting in less amnesia.

Next in line is the *complex and structured* category, which includes client systems that rate as moderately complex, moderately structured, poorly to moderately organized, and having rigid dissociative barriers. Responsible adults are less likely to be well-defined. The primary difference between this category and the previous one is that complex and structured client systems will have at least one more layer or level of alters, which are often unknown or only partially known by the client. As therapy progresses and a significant amount of communication, cooperation, and co-consciousness develops among the top level of alters, it becomes more likely that some of the alters in the next level will reveal themselves. When they do, it will be likely that they will appear dangerous. They may be full of rage or wanting to seek revenge. Some may be child alters who have been abandoned. Fortunately, with better

* Colin Ross (1999) notes that this is considered normal in our culture, but he critiques this stance as due to a "lack of fluidity in the psyche" and refers to it as "pathological pseudounity" (p. 194).

cohesion in the top layer, the system will be better prepared to welcome the emerging alters from the lower layers in a safe way, providing the reeducation and nurturing that the lower-layer alters will need.

The final category is the *complex and unstructured* system, in which clients have a chaotic and unpredictable system. Somehow, the client is able to function in the outer world while their inner world remains fluid and sometimes shifts uncontrollably. The alters do not seem to have clear roles. Clients with this system would rate close to a 1 on the first six attributes of the dimensional model. As you explore this inner world during therapy, it is difficult to get a handle on what is actually happening because the alters and the inner landscape keep shifting and changing without a clear reason why. These systems will often have many layers of alters. Many clients with this sort of system have suffered ritualistic abuse. The clients fitting into this category will be the most difficult and challenging to work with.

The dimensional and categorical scales offered here are guideposts, not permanent fixtures, and they may not be beneficial for every client with OSDD or DID. How your client perceives and understands their own system is more important than your conceptualization of it. At any rate, you can utilize the ten aspirations and three foundational pillars in therapy regardless of how the client system is organized.

CHAPTER 6

COMMUNICATION, COOPERATION, AND CO-CONSCIOUSNESS: THE THIRD PILLAR

Therapists working with clients with DID are faced at the beginning of treatment with a fundamental paradox. The trauma that clients with DID experienced in childhood was intolerable and required an ingenious solution: the creation of alternate identities or alters. The memories and pain of abuse and neglect held by one alter could then be hidden from other alters through a dissociative barrier. Alters who remained unaware of the abuse were free to interact with their abusers without getting overwhelmed with traumatic memories. Overall, the fragmentation served as a successful strategy for survival, which is why clients with DID, at least initially, will usually find it too dangerous to forfeit in therapy.

The paradox comes to play in that the chaotic life experienced by many clients with DID is caused by the rigidity of those very dissociative barriers, and successful therapy requires, at the very least, a loosening of those barriers. Alters with rigid dissociative barriers do not have the capacity to communicate with each other. They can take charge of the body on a whim, interact with other people, form relationships, spend money, and engage in risky behaviors without the other alters in the system being aware of what is going on.

If the breakdown of those barriers occurs too quickly through the therapeutic process, there is a risk that the client will decompensate, resulting in rapid switching, self-harm, alcohol or drug usage, and suicidality. So, the dilemma is as follows: The dissociative barriers need to begin to dissolve in order for the therapy to be successful, but the act of dissolution is likely to make the client worse, at least in the short term. The three Cs is the solution to this dilemma. There will still be obstacles and setbacks, and the risk of retraumatization and decompensation is still very real, but the three Cs allows for the dissolution of these dissociative barriers to occur slowly and carefully, with the client system in charge of that process.

One of the first tasks in developing the three Cs is to name them as therapeutic goals. I recommend that you simply tell your clients that the three Cs—inner communication, cooperation, and co-consciousness—are essential for successful outcomes of therapy. It is unrealistic, however, to expect clients with DID to immediately agree to the three Cs as therapeutic goals since fragmentation and secrecy have been essential for their survival. Indeed, clients often perceive the three Cs as frightening and dangerous in the early stages of the work. Therefore, rather than trying to convince clients of how essential the three Cs are, a gentle approach is necessary. Introducing the three Cs as goals early on may serve to plant seeds that will sprout and grow as the therapeutic process moves forward.

COMMUNICATION

When it comes to communication, alters with strong dissociative barriers are unwilling, and believe they are unable, to communicate with each other. However, if you are acutely perceptive, there is often evidence of the opposite. For example, let's say you are working with a client named George, who has been diagnosed with DID. It is early in the therapy process, and you are aware of three alters: George, the primary alter and the responsible adult who comes to therapy; Genevieve, a female teenager protector alter; and Georgette, a female child alter. George comes for his appointment on a Thursday and reports that he remembers going to bed on Tuesday night and waking up on Thursday morning, with total amnesia for the whole day Wednesday.

You ask George if he is curious about what happened on Wednesday, and he says he is. You then ask George if he would be willing to close his eyes and check in with Genevieve and Georgette to see if they could tell him what happened on Wednesday. George replies there is zero communication with either of them. He is sure that Genevieve doesn't wish to talk to him, and Georgette cries a lot and is too young to be able to speak anyway.

At this point, you might notice that you've been struck by another paradox. On the one hand, George says he has no communication with either Genevieve or Georgette. On the other hand, he somehow has the knowledge that Genevieve doesn't want to talk to him and that little Georgette cries a lot and hasn't learned to talk yet. George is an intelligent person, but he is unable to see the contradiction. He doesn't allow himself to realize that Genevieve must have communicated her unwillingness to talk to George, or he otherwise wouldn't be aware of the fact, and that Georgette's crying is also a form of communication.

It is your job to point out these paradoxes to the client. You could say, "I'm curious as to how you discovered that Genevieve doesn't want to talk to you." In response, George might say that he could just feel it. You may then provide some psychoeducation around the issue of communication, explaining that it doesn't always have to be in words and can occur as a feeling, a sense, or a knowingness. Once you've planted the idea that Genevieve did in fact communicate to George through her feelings, you could ask him whether he could distinguish what the feeling was—for example, anger, sadness, or fear.

COOPERATION

As communication between alters gets established, cooperation becomes possible. Initially, the cooperation can be very simple. In the previous example, once Genevieve learns to communicate her feelings to George, many opportunities emerge for you to ask helpful questions. Could George check in with Genevieve and ask her to share what she was feeling on Wednesday? What was Georgette's crying all about? When George hears Georgette crying, could he reach out to comfort her or perhaps ask Genevieve to do so? In doing so, you facilitate two possible therapeutic outcomes:

1. **You find out what happened Wednesday:** The importance of this cannot be underestimated. You can assume that this is not the first time George has experienced lost time, nor will it be the last. It is next to impossible to have stability in life if at any point, without any preparation or awareness, hours or days can go by where a client is engaging in activities without the primary alter knowing what is happening.
2. **The client system begins to become aware of itself:** In a healthy DID system, there is enough of a hierarchy that the responsible adult makes important life decisions, including which alter fronts the body at any given time. A reasonably functioning inner communication system exists. Every alter is listened to, honored, and respected for the role they play in the system. The inner children are taken care of. Disputes are resolved through communication and cooperation. These outcomes will not occur by accident, and it is not enough for you to simply have

a discussion with George about the lost time on Wednesday to achieve all these aspirations. However, in the best of circumstances, it will help the client system move closer to these goals.

CO-CONSCIOUSNESS

The third C, co-consciousness, requires an additional explanation. It occurs when there is one alter fronting the body while another alter stays nearby and is aware of what is happening. It is highly advantageous for clients to learn this skill, as it greatly reduces the experience of lost time. It isn't necessary for every alter to develop this ability, but it is especially important for the responsible adults to do so. When a responsible adult alter has the ability to stay close by and monitor the situation in the event that the system gets triggered and a different alter takes over the body, this reduces the chances of dire consequences. This works best when the responsible adult is able to communicate with the alter who has taken over or, in the case of a crisis, push the other alter aside and retake control over the body.

For example, consider a scenario where you are talking to a primary alter named Daniel. Daniel informs you that a child alter named Danny wishes to come out and meet you. After checking for safety and ground rules, you ask Daniel to stay close by and listen in on the conversation while Danny takes over control of the body. While talking to Danny, you ask him if he can sense Daniel's presence. If he can't, you would ask Daniel to come closer so Danny can sense him. You can then facilitate a conversation between Daniel and Danny while Danny is in control of the body. If this is successful, it could be said that Daniel and Danny had an experience of co-consciousness. Developing the skill of co-consciousness takes time, so it is helpful for you to encourage clients to practice this in between sessions.

At the extreme end of the co-consciousness continuum, two or more alters can develop the ability to work together in occupying the body. They may take turns in deciding on moment-to-moment actions and choices, or they may develop a kind of groupthink, whereby they are in concert as they move through their day. In a sense, they may merge together from time to time and then separate as needed, depending on what the current occasion presents. When a client with DID has advanced to this point in their healing, it is possible that the merging may become permanent.

You can see an example of this merging in the following scenario. Suppose you are working with a client system that has three responsible adult alters: Mary, Maria, and Christina. Mary is considered the primary alter: the one who attends therapy and interacts with her partner and friends. Maria is the alter who was trained as an office assistant. She's the one who goes to work every day, has work friends, and handles all the work responsibilities, as well as keeping track of household bills and appointments. Christina is a teenage protector alter. In the early stages of therapy, Christina has a difficult time learning to trust you, and she objects whenever Mary wants to share memories of childhood abuse.

Through the therapeutic process, you honor Christina's needs whenever she expresses a concern, and you make sure to slow down the pace of sharing. In turn, Christina begins to trust you and, over time, has less reason to protect the system. She adopts the three Cs as her own special project and encourages the other alters to share and work together. When she finally shares her own memories of abuse and goes through a special session to process and heal from those experiences (as you will read about in chapter 11), Christina "ages up" from her teenage status to an adult and joins Mary and Maria as responsible adult alters. She then takes on the responsibility of advising Mary and Maria when they find themselves in dangerous situations at work or in their personal life.

In this scenario, you can see that Mary, Maria, and Christina were able to break down the barriers that separated them through a process of sharing their unique memories with each other. As those dissociative barriers dissolved, their identities naturally began to coalesce.

THE THERAPIST AS A HISTORIAN

Especially in the early stages of therapy, it is helpful for you to ask at the beginning of each session what the client remembers about the previous session. The answer to this question provides a wealth of information: how much lost time the client may be experiencing, what the client's switching process looks like, and who tends to be fronting the body when the client comes to therapy. This will often lead to conversations that promote the three Cs. In this way, you play an important role as an historian who reminds the client of what was discussed in the last session and you bring the client back to the three Cs.

For example, let's say that George describes the lost Wednesday incident as a "one-time thing" and says you shouldn't be concerned about it. But if this was actually the tenth time that you've explored the experience of lost time with George, then you, as a historian, would remind him of that. Incidents such as this don't necessarily mean that the client is purposely deceiving you, although that is certainly possible. More likely, further exploration will reveal that a different alter was present, pretending to be the primary, and did not have any memories of the other occasions of lost time. This discovery will be important in the goal of getting to know the alters and the switching process.

RETRAUMATIZATION

As clients begin to develop the three Cs, you need to be alert to the possibility of retraumatization and decompensation. While the dissolution of dissociative barriers is essential for successful outcomes, breaking down those walls too quickly can cause locked-away secrets and painful traumatic memories to flood an unprepared system. Resourcing, the first pillar, along with the default position of slowing things down, provides the necessary antidote to this flooding. As clients enhance their inner communication and cooperation skills, they can set up a plan for certain alters to monitor the risk of flooding. With your assistance, when retraumatization does occur, you can help the client implement resourcing skills to deal with the crisis.

Unfortunately, in the mental health world of today, there are pressures on therapists from insurance companies, governmental bodies, and even private practice agencies to increase productivity. As therapists, we often respond to those pressures by moving clients though our systems as quickly as possible to make room for the next set of clients. This means we are essentially attempting to identify problems, agree on treatment plans with goals and objectives, and plan for discharge as soon as we begin therapy. Working with clients with DID requires that we let go of the desire to move quickly, as the best antidote to retraumatization and decompensation is to slow down the process. Aspiration 7 is relevant here: "Trust the process rather than focusing on your expectations for the outcome."

Fortunately, the three Cs provide a way for you to ease through the dissociative barriers slowly and safely. As alters begin to talk to each other and learn to cooperate in problem-solving activities, and as periods of co-consciousness increase, the dissociative barriers begin to lessen in an organic, safe manner. Nevertheless, bottom-up therapeutic modalities, such as EMDR and CRM, can be powerfully effective in resolving trauma memories. However, the risk of utilizing these modalities too soon and without adequate preparation is that the dissociative barriers dissolve too quickly. This can throw the system into crisis, allowing for rapid switching to occur and increasing the risk that violent protector alters or suicidal alters will take control. In order to reduce these risks, I recommend that you make certain preparations, which I describe in chapter 11.

Buy-in for the three Cs doesn't occur all at once. In the beginning, the three Cs are operating to some degree, but the client is unaware of it. When you point out those incidents and encourage the system to enhance those skills, the client may resist at first. Over time, though, the client will hopefully learn that developing these skills results in a calmer, less chaotic life. When the client buys in fully to the three Cs, the system will take steps (often two steps forward and one step back) to achieve these goals. The process continues throughout the entire treatment process.

MOVING BETWEEN THE THREE PILLARS

Clinical judgment, along with a keen curiosity and a commitment to centering the client system, will determine which of the three pillars becomes the initial focus in any particular therapeutic session. Regardless of which pillar you explore first, it is important to always notice the other two pillars standing nearby, ready to be brought into the conversation.

For example, let's say a client begins a session recounting a recent traumatic experience. As the client shares what happened, you notice that they are beginning to become emotionally activated, so you invite them to practice a breathing exercise they learned in a previous session, which reflects resourcing (pillar 1). As the client closes their eyes and begins the process, their body trembles briefly. Their eyes open, and a protective alter takes over. In turn, you express curiosity as to who has emerged, which reflects your shift to getting to know the alters (pillar 2). The client responds by saying they don't know who they are, so you invite them to look inside and see if they can talk to the alter whom they just replaced. In this respect, you have now switched your focus to the three Cs (pillar 3), specifically inner communication.

As the session continues, you and the client move around in a circle—engaging one pillar, then another, and then another. It becomes seamless, as all three pillars are necessary in doing DID therapeutic work. Once you become proficient in facilitating these three pillars, a fluidity develops whereby the three pillars and the three aspects of each pillar begin to work together without requiring that you consciously choose one pillar over another. It may be helpful to think of the three pillars as legs on a three-legged stool. If you remove just one of the legs, the stool cannot stand.

CHAPTER 7

DEVELOPMENTAL TRAUMA AND ATTACHMENT WOUNDS

In order to understand how DID develops, it is first necessary to understand the effects of early childhood trauma and insecure attachment (Ross, 2000). As humans, we are born helpless. We cannot feed ourselves, soothe ourselves, or manage any of our survival needs. Like all mammals, we are wired to attach to someone who can take care of us, usually a mother or another adult; this need reflects an external locus of control in that the attachment figure has the control. While infants will work hard to get their mother's attention by turning toward her, seeking eye contact, fussing, crying, or wailing, the mother ultimately decides whether and how to respond. Whenever these attempts for attention are not successful, the baby will become distressed, but as long as the baby's actions result in getting their needs met most of the time, the occasional distress the baby feels will not be overwhelming, and the baby will develop a secure attachment.

When the only available adult is inattentive, emotionally absent, or a perpetrator, the child's need for attachment remains, but the attachment becomes problematic. The perpetrator's abuse or neglect results in the child becoming overwhelmed by pain and a sense of powerlessness. The child can't stop the experiences from happening, can't control what happens, and can't even predict when it will happen. In these circumstances, withdrawing from the perpetrator is impossible since the child still needs this attachment figure to survive. The result of this situation is the development of an insecure form of attachment, either the avoidant type, which often manifests as emotional aloofness in adulthood, or the ambivalent type, which often manifests as clinging, dependent behavior in adulthood.

At any rate, the child must find a way to decrease their sense of powerlessness and pain, as it is not sustainable, so they decide that the problem doesn't reside in the attachment figure but in themselves. They develop a narrative of "I am a bad person. That's why I am being abused," which reflects a locus of control shift. On the surface, this shift represents a seemingly elegant solution to the child's dilemma. Now the child can spend time working on becoming good. The child learns to listen carefully to the attachment figure to sense their moods and try to predict their actions. The child tries everything possible to please the attachment figure. However, when the child inevitably fails in these attempts, this reinforces the belief that there is something terribly bad about them. In this way, the internal locus of control shift is amplified. For survivors of serious trauma, it can be especially difficult to let go of the belief in their inherent "badness."

Children who go on to develop dissociative identities in response to such trauma likely have a genetic predisposition that gives them a greater capacity for dissociation than others (ISSTD, 2011). Moreover, while children with dissociative tendencies also experience the locus of control shift, the abuse and neglect they suffer is generally so severe and unpredictable that this shift is insufficient to resolve it. They must continue approaching their attachment figure for survival, but to do so is likely to produce more abuse, creating a no-win situation. Their solution is dissociation, coinciding with a form of insecure attachment known as the disorganized type, which manifests as a mix of anxious and ambivalent behavior in adulthood.

Let's take, for example, a child who is sexually abused during the night and is expected to get up in the morning and get ready for school as if nothing happened. One way to succeed in this task is to create a different identity who doesn't recall the abuse and can get ready for school without feeling the anguish of the night's events. This is accomplished by creating a dissociative barrier between the identity who experiences the abuse and the identity who goes to school. Neither is aware of the other's existence.

This scenario is then repeated over and over again. For example, the child may be abused by different perpetrators, with each experience requiring a different identity to learn to tolerate the abuse and creating additional dissociative barriers. As the child masters this creative ability, they can use it for other situations as well. One identity might focus on math skills, another on history lessons. One might become good at peer friendships, another at caring for their younger siblings. One might imitate the perpetrator and focus on self-harm behaviors as a way to please the perpetrator. Another might decide that suicide is the only viable option.

What initially developed as a creative survival method becomes problematic as the child grows into adulthood and is hopefully no longer subject to the abusive situations. Rapid switching from one identity to another with amnesia can create a chaotic adulthood. It is helpful to note that many clients with DID retain the ability to create new alters in adulthood when experiencing new traumatic events. This should be discouraged, as it increases the complexity of the system and creates more problems than it solves.

THE TRAUMA CYCLE

Individuals who have experienced trauma, especially complex childhood trauma, often get caught in a cycle involving three stages. First, they go through life feeling numb, which often manifests as depression. In order to feel alive again and find relief, they seek out intense experiences, whether that's using alcohol, drugs, or other substances, or engaging in other self-harming behaviors. They may also subject themselves to unsafe places and practices that result in further abuse from others. These actions then lead the client to experience retraumatization, which leads to a numbing of emotions and shutting down, and the cycle repeats itself (see figure 4).

Figure 4: The Trauma Cycle

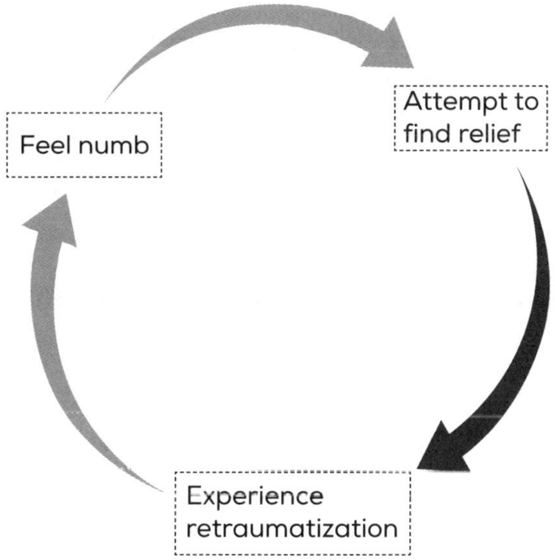

Feel numb

Attempt to find relief

Experience retraumatization

To assist trauma survivors in stepping out of the trauma cycle, you must first provide psychoeducation explaining how the process works. Then, as the client shares distressing experiences that fit within the cycle, you can refer back to the information you have shared. For example, let's say you are working with a client who suffered abuse in childhood at the hands of her father and, as a result, she frequently struggles with self-harm. If this client comes to session one week describing how numb she feels, as her historian, you can remind her of potential triggers for this numbness—for example, she was retraumatized last week by the anniversary of her father's death—and ask her if this could be an example of the trauma cycle in operation. This won't immediately resolve the issue, but over time, the client will hopefully be able to predict the next step in the cycle, prepare herself for it, and eventually minimize its effect. In this example, you can remind the client that if she stays in the cycle, she is likely to engage in self-harm behavior to find relief from the numbing.

To complicate the process even further for clients with DID, there may be alters who are perpetually depressed, others who are reckless, and still others who are caught in the reenactment of past trauma. In the previous example, there could be a child alter in the client's system who remains stuck in the memory of the abuse. When retraumatized by the anniversary of her father's death, the child alter causes the body to go numb. This, in turn, empowers another alter, one who knows that harming the body is an antidote to the numbness, to emerge. The self-harming behavior is in itself traumatizing, resulting in a return of the numbness. As each of these alters takes over fronting the body, the cycle continues and is difficult to stop. Besides reminding clients like this of the ways the cycle tends to work, you can also focus on the second pillar (getting to know the alters) and the third pillar (the three Cs), and facilitate communication among the alters involved in aspects of the cycle. You can ensure each alter is aware of the role they are playing in the cycle and enlist their support in stepping away from their usual behavior in order to support the system.

VICTIM-PERPETRATOR-RESCUER TRIANGLE

Children who experience abuse are forced onto a triangle characterized by the following roles: (1) the victim, who represents the client; (2) the perpetrator, who represents their abuser; and (3) the rescuer, who represents the individual who extricated the client from the abusive experience, or in cases where no one rescued the child, there is always an imaginary rescuer (Ross, 2000). Due to the sustaining power of these experiences, this triangle of roles will often become embedded into the brains of clients so much so that it is simply the way the world works. As adults, they tend to view other people as embodying one of the points of this triangle. This can become problematic for clients who are attempting to live fulfilling lives with nurturing relationships. They may, for example, identify with the victim role and seek out relationships with others who are more than happy to step into the perpetrator role. Others may identify with the rescuer role and spend most of their time and energy trying to save others who are in trouble, neglecting their own needs and abandoning any semblance of self-care. They might even identify with the perpetrator role and become abusers themselves.

All of the above is relevant to any client with early childhood trauma, but for those with DID, it becomes even more complicated, as they may have alters who identity with each of these roles. For example, they can have alters who identify with the perpetrator role and spend time putting down the other alters. They can also have alters who identify with the victim role. Often, these are child alters who hide away inside the system, reexperiencing the trauma. There can also be alters who see themselves as rescuers. These alters can, at least initially, be helpful to the system as they may work diligently to take care of the little ones or organize the client's schedule.

What often becomes problematic is when the therapeutic relationship reenacts a perpetrator-victim-rescuer triangle, which can happen with both the client and the therapist being unaware of it. For example, consider a situation in which your client recounts a horrendous experience of abuse and names their stepfather as the perpetrator. It is easy for the client to recruit you into stepping into the role of rescuer, but if you refuse to do so, the client may shift their perspective and view you as the perpetrator. When this happens, they are likely to seek out someone else to be the rescuer by asking for a different therapist. Alternatively, the client might become angry at you and adopt the role of the perpetrator by lashing out verbally at you. If you aren't careful, you might begin to see yourself as the victim. Around and around the triangle you go.

The only way out of this dilemma is to, as early as possible, become aware that the client is reenacting the triangle and to step away from it all together. Reenactment of abuse is not therapy. As long as you find yourself in the triangle, regardless of whether you're a perpetrator, victim, or rescuer, therapy has ceased, and you are experiencing countertransference. It takes a great deal of awareness and skill to refuse to allow yourself to get caught in this triangle, and if you are caught, to immediately extricate yourself from it. Seeking consultation from a supervisor or trusted peer can be helpful in these situations, and if the countertransference is serious enough, seeking your own therapy may be necessary.

THE RELIABILITY OF MEMORY

In the 1980s and early 1990s, some mental health therapists employed a strategy called "recovered memory therapy" as a way to help clients to retrieve repressed memories of childhood abuse. For example, therapists pressured clients to recall traumatic childhood experiences while strongly suggesting the outcome they expected. In other words, vulnerable clients, often in a hypnotic trance, were fed misinformation in the form of suggestions by someone they trusted as an authority figure. In response, Dr. Elizabeth Loftus and others (1995) conducted a series of scientific studies demonstrating that under conditions such as these, false memories can be implanted. There was evidence of occasions when recovered memory therapy did in fact result in false memories of abuse, which resulted in a public debate between experimental psychologists and mental health practitioners, dubbed the "memory wars."

Neuroscientist Charan Ranganath's (2024) book *Why We Remember* argues that media coverage of the memory wars distorted the research by falsely claiming that we can never trust our memories of past events. He asserts that clients can in fact accurately remember many aspects of traumatic memories and that responsible therapists today are careful not to reproduce the specific conditions used in recovered memory therapy that can lead to false memories. Indeed, as I discuss in chapter 11, except for some gentle inquiries about childhood trauma during initial assessments, I do not recommend asking clients for detailed information concerning their memories of abuse, much less pressuring them to remember. It is also important to keep your focus on the ten aspirations, which provide strong protection against false memories, especially the following: "Foster an abundance of curiosity regarding the client's system" (aspiration 4) and "Trust the process rather than focusing on your expectations for the outcome" (aspiration 7).

Unfortunately, one result of the memory wars is that many mental health providers have been scared away from facing the frequency of childhood trauma and its devastating effects throughout the life cycle. Some of these fears remain with us today with the belief that DID is rare or too weird to be true. As a result, "trauma survivors have become collateral damage in the memory wars" (Ranganath, 2024, p. 151).

Still, a nuanced view of memory is warranted because, even in the best of circumstances, human memory is unreliable. Every time we recall an event from our past, the memory changes. The details and sequence of the event may change, as well as the emotional intensity, or lack thereof, attached to the memory (O'Keane, 2021). This raises an important consideration when working with clients with early childhood trauma in general, and with clients with DID in particular. Many childhood trauma survivors have, at some point in time, told someone what happened in the hopes of getting help, and they were not believed. If they were believed, they may have been blamed for the abuse that happened to them. In turn, when and if they find the courage to share one of those painful memories with you, they desperately want to be acknowledged and believed. They may even ask, "Do you believe me?"

The challenge is to acknowledge and authenticate the reality of the client's traumatic experience without subscribing to all the details of the memory. This becomes especially true when working with clients with DID. For example, consider a scenario in which a primary alter, Hanna, shares a memory with you in which she was abused by her grandfather, and she desperately wishes for you to believe her story. However, another alter named Erik then appears, who also wishes to be believed. Erik says, "Yes we were abused, but it wasn't by our grandfather—it was in fact by our great-uncle." There is no way for you to know which account is correct, if both are true, or if both could be mistaken. Maybe it was the client's older brother or a next-door neighbor who wore a mask and pretended to be the grandfather, the uncle, or both.

Alter conflicts and disagreements are inevitable, and it is a mistake for you to take sides in these conflicts. The best strategy is to anticipate these memory differences and bring up the issue early in the therapeutic relationship. The following dialogue describes one example of how you can accomplish this:

Therapist: Before we get too far in our work together, I would like to talk about memory, if that's okay with you.

Hanna: Okay, that's fine.

Therapist: You've already told me that there are lots of things that happened in your childhood that you don't remember.

Hanna: That's right. That's not so unusual, is it?

Therapist: No, not unusual at all, especially for people like yourself who have experienced childhood trauma.

Hanna: I'm not so sure I want to try to drag up those memories.

Therapist: I agree. I just wanted to let you know that even when we do remember something from our childhood, it is unlikely that our memory will be totally accurate.

Hanna: Why is that?

Therapist: Several reasons. If the memory is of a traumatic event, the part of our brain that creates the memory won't be functioning very well. Certain details of the event may be strong, but other details may be absent or remembered inaccurately.

Hanna: I didn't know that.

Therapist: Things that you're told about the event later can change the memory as well. Just thinking about the event can change some aspects of the memory. Since you have other alters, you might also remember certain details of the event, and other alters might remember other details. You and the other alters might also remember the same details completely differently from one another.

Hanna: Sounds complicated.

Therapist: I want you to know that I will help you sort these things out. If other alters have different views of a memory, I will respect each one's perspective and won't take sides, because I will understand the suffering you all experienced.

The therapist and Hanna continue working together over the next two months, during which time they both learn more details about the client system and the alters who are active. For example, Erik is a protector who is often critical toward Hanna. He also is influential with the other alters in the inner realm. There is also a six-year-old child alter named Crystal, who was found hiding under a bed in a hidden bedroom in the inner world, and a teenager named Daniele who babysits Crystal. Hanna is just beginning to learn to communicate with Erik but has refused to interact with Crystal. Erik, in turn, is emotionally abusive toward Crystal.

Therapist: At the end of our last session, you indicated that you wanted to talk a little about your grandfather. Is he your paternal or maternal grandfather?

Hanna: Actually, he is my mother's second husband's father, but he lived with us for a time, and everyone called him Gramps.

Therapist: How old were you when he lived with your family?

Hanna: I'm not sure, around the age of six to ten.

Therapist: What was he like?

Hanna: He was an asshole, if you want to know, and he abused me. [*She closes her eyes and holds her head down.*]

Therapist: Hanna, I can see you are having strong feelings right now. We can go at your own pace, and we don't have to talk about what happened if you aren't ready.

Crystal: [*She wrings her hands together.*] No Hanna.

Therapist: Oh, hi there. What's your name?

Crystal: [*She whispers, looking down.*] Crystal.

Therapist: I'm happy to meet you. Hanna told me a little about you.

Crystal: I'm scared.

Therapist: It's okay, Crystal. Do you know who I am?

Crystal: I have to go now. [*She closes her eyes.*]

Therapist: Okay. Thanks for coming out to meet me.

Erik: [*He opens his eyes.*] Now you've really done it.

Therapist: Hello there. Who am I speaking to?

Erik: You're not doing so well today, doc. First you made Hanna cry. Then you made Crystal come out. [*This reflects one of the three Cs—inner communication.*]

Therapist: Erik?

Erik: Yeah, it's me.

Therapist: I apologize. Perhaps my questions were too intrusive. Can you check in to see if Hanna and Crystal are okay?

Erik: Crystal is fine. Daniele is looking after her. I don't really care about Hanna because she's a big liar.

Therapist: Would you mind checking in with Hanna anyway, and let her know I apologize for pushing too hard?

Erik: Fine. [*He closes his eyes for a moment, then opens them again.*] Aren't you worried that Hanna is a big liar?

Therapist: Can you explain more about this?

Erik: It's simple. Hanna told you that Gramps abused us, but that's a lie. It was our uncle. Gramps was a mean SOB, but he'd never do anything sexual.

Therapist: Is it possible that you and Hanna remember the event differently?

Erik: No, I remember it clearly. I don't know why, but she's lying about it, and I thought you should know it. That's the only reason I came out today.

Therapist: I appreciate you coming out to talk to me, but do you remember a conversation I had with Hanna a couple months ago about how memory can be unreliable?

Erik: I don't have time to listen in on every stupid conversation you have with Hanna.

Therapist: Okay. I understand. I can give you the highlights if you want.

Erik: If you must.

Therapist: I explained to Hanna that memory is often inaccurate in the best of times. For folks with more than one identity, it can be even less accurate.

Erik: Why would that be?

Therapist: For example, you don't remember the conversation I just had with Hanna because Hanna was fronting the body then, and for some reason or another, you weren't listening. If I asked you what you remembered about that day, your memory would be very different from Hanna's.

Erik: Okay, I guess that makes sense.

Therapist: When you were abused, there may have been times when you were fronting the body and other times when Hanna was, so you remember different things.

Erik: I still know what I know. Do you believe me, or do you believe the liar Hanna?

Therapist: I believe you were abused, but I have no way of knowing which details are correct in your memory, or in Hanna's.

Erik: I'm not talking about details. I'm talking about who did it, and who didn't do it.

Therapist: I hear you, Erik. My job is to help both of you heal from the trauma. It would be harmful for me to believe it was your uncle and consider Hanna a liar, or believe it was Gramps and call you a liar.

Erik: I don't think you can be neutral in this case, doc.

Therapist: I understand what you are saying, that it may appear I am being neutral. I want to emphasize though that I am totally against the abuse you all suffered, and I will be here for you, Hanna, and any other alters who are part of your system.

Erik: If that's the best you can do.

Therapist: Thanks for coming out to talk, and thanks for sharing. Would you be willing to check in to see how Hanna is doing now and if she would be willing to come back out so I can talk to her a few minutes before the end of our meeting today? [*Erik closes his eyes.*]

Hanna: [*She opens her eyes.*] I'm back. I'm sorry I left like that. What happened?

Therapist: Erik came out to talk to me.

Hanna: Really? What did he say?

Therapist: He was upset about what you said about Gramps. He remembered it differently. He said it was your uncle and not Gramps who was the abuser.

Hanna: So which one of us do you believe?

Therapist: Do you remember talking with me a couple months ago about how memories are often not accurate?

Hanna: Vaguely.

Therapist: I believe you were abused, but there is no way for me to know which one of you has a more accurate memory. I won't ever take sides between the alters in your system. In either case, I will be here to help all of you to heal from your traumatic experiences.

Hanna: I'm kind of tired.

Therapist: Our time is about up now anyway, but before you go, could you check in with Daniele to see how Crystal is doing? I don't know if you were listening, but she did come out for a few minutes to meet me. She was pretty scared though.

Hanna: Okay. [*She is silent for a few moments.*] It's hard for me to connect with Daniele, who is watching her, but I think Crystal is fine. I'm surprised she came out.

Therapist: I'm wondering if it was because I asked you about Gramps. I apologize if I was pushing too hard with my questions.

Hanna: Not your fault. I think it was Erik interfering.

Therapist: We can slow things down. I'm glad Crystal has Daniele to look after her. Do you think, eventually, you could get to know Daniele better?

Hanna: Not sure about that, but I guess I can try.

Therapist: Let me know next week how it goes.

Hanna: Will do. Bye.

In spite of the therapist's preparation, this example leaves things hanging. They will need to have further conversations to deal with the loss of trust and attunement. It is possible that other alters may emerge to mediate the conflict between Hanna and Erik. At any rate, it is not the therapist's responsibility to ascertain which memories are accurate and which ones are not. As mentioned earlier, all memories are suspect due to their inherent unreliability. Aspiration 8 is relevant here: "Be acutely aware of your own limitations and share with your client when appropriate." None of this, however, takes away from the therapeutic goals of healing from past trauma. By returning to the three pillars, we can see that even in this difficult session, much work was done in getting to know Erik, Hanna, Crystal, and even a little about Daniele. The three Cs were also engaged. In chapter 11, I'll discuss how to process trauma memories in greater detail.

CHAPTER 8

PSYCHOEDUCATION

Psychoeducation is an important part of almost all therapeutic endeavors. For clients with DID, there are several considerations regarding how much information to provide, when to offer it, how to provide it, and for what purpose. This would be true for all clients, whether diagnosed with DID or not. In general, the amount of psychoeducation you provide should be determined by how curious the client is about certain features of the work. Sometimes, clients will ask particular questions that make this easy to determine. For example, a client may ask, "How is therapy going to help me?"

It is your responsibility to answer this question using language that is likely to make sense for the client based on their educational background and intellectual level. You could start with a general statement such as "Sometimes it helps to talk about problems and concerns with someone who will listen closely." Depending on the client's response, you could offer more detailed information. Here is a dialogue that illustrates this how this might play out:

Noah: How is therapy going to help me?

Therapist: Sometimes it helps to talk about problems and concerns with someone who will listen closely.

Noah: I don't see how just talking is going to resolve anything. We can talk and talk, but when I walk out of your office, the problems in my life will still be there.

Therapist: I agree that talking to me won't solve your problems unless it leads to you finding new ways to actually make changes in your life.

Noah: And you can help me with that?

Therapist: Yes. There are two ways that can happen. First, you might get new ideas from our discussions, and then try out those ideas. Second, our work together might result in changes in the way you interpret events in your life, which could give you more options and help you make different choices.

Noah: Worth a try, I guess. My main problem is the way my girlfriend treats me.

In this case, the client communicates that he has heard enough psychoeducation and is ready to begin working on problems. Alternatively, consider a situation in which the client answers this way:

Noah: I've had lots of therapy in the past and have tried making different choices, but nothing ever works out. How will this be any different?

Therapist: That's a really good question. Every therapist is different, with their own style, their own educational level, and their own unique skills.

At this point, the therapist would probably be curious about the client's past experiences in therapy, including what kinds of things he has already tried and what changes he really wants to make. If, at some point in the conversation, the client were to become curious about the change process itself, the therapist could provide additional psychoeducation.

DISSOCIATION AND DIAGNOSIS

Dissociation is often misunderstood, stereotyped, and dismissed, even by clinicians, so it is not surprising that clients, including those who experience it every day, are often unaware of what it is. Providing psychoeducation on dissociation is important when assessing new clients whom you suspect may have DID as well as those you have already diagnosed. It is initially helpful to normalize the experience. For example, you might point out that spacing out when driving, which is called *highway hypnosis*, is actually a form of dissociation. So is being caught up in a television show or video game so much so that you don't hear when someone calls your name. Experiencing flashbacks, which is common among soldiers with PTSD, is a more serious form of dissociation, as is losing significant blocks of time.

Once you have normalized dissociation, clients may be more comfortable discussing their experiences. This is especially the case for clients who routinely lose blocks of time and have amnesia regarding what occurred during those periods. These clients often find ways to minimize these experiences, which may be an unconscious strategy that allows them to avoid facing the extent of their multiplicity. When you express your curiosity regarding these missing blocks of time, clients may feel freer to address it. If therapy has progressed to the point where multiple alters are in communication with the primary, then you can encourage the primary to talk to other alters who may be able to fill in the blanks in their memory. The following dialogue between a therapist and a client demonstrates one possible way to provide helpful psychoeducation around this important issue:

Therapist: [*The therapist normalizes dissociation, as described previously, before continuing.*] One way to think about dissociation is on a continuum, with normal dissociation such as highway hypnosis on one end, and severe dissociation on the other end, where a person has separate identities who take over the body from time to time. Where do you think you might fit on this continuum?

Noah: Probably somewhere in the middle.

Therapist: Are there times when you lose a block of time?

Noah: Well, sometimes I space out and something happens and I don't remember what I did.

Therapist: How often does this happen?

Noah: I think I space out a lot, but usually I remember what happened.

Therapist: Does it worry you when you don't remember? [*This question is important because it is common for clients with DID to fill in the gaps and avoid trying to find out what occurred while they suffered amnesia.*]

Noah: Now that we are talking about it, it does seem important, but at the time, I try to push it aside and not worry about it.

Therapist: Has it ever happened to you that not remembering caused you some additional problems?

Noah: Like what?

Therapist: Oh, I don't know. Maybe you got embarrassed because someone was upset with you for something, but you didn't even remember what you did.

Noah: Maybe they are the one making things up.

Therapist: Sure, that could happen. [*Noah pauses, but the therapist resists the urge to say something, providing time and space for him to reflect inwardly, which supports inner communication, part of the three Cs.*]

Noah: There was one time. It was with my girlfriend.

Therapist: If you want to talk about it, I'm listening.

Noah: We were arguing in the living room, then the next thing I knew, I was sitting in the kitchen, and I don't remember going in there. I got up and looked around for my girlfriend and she wasn't in the apartment.

Therapist: It sounds like you lost a block of time. Does that make sense to you?

Noah: It doesn't make sense, but I think that's what happened.

Therapist: Did you talk to your girlfriend later about it?

Noah: Not really. When she came home, she wouldn't talk to me at all. The next day she just told me if I ever did that again, she would leave me.

Therapist: Did you find out what you did?

Noah: No, I just told her I was sorry and it would never happen again.

Therapist: Weren't you curious about what you did?

Noah: At the time, I didn't want her to say because I had no way to know if she would be telling the truth or lying about it.

Therapist: What are your thoughts about it now?

Noah: I'm not stupid. How could I promise not to do something, when I didn't even know what I did?

Therapist: Okay. If you want, we could talk more about lost time and what causes it.

Noah: Okay, I guess.

Therapist: Do you have any idea how much time you lost?

Noah: Not sure, an hour or two maybe.

Therapist: Do you have a theory as to what caused you to lose time?

Noah: All I can say is I must have spaced out.

Therapist: While you were spaced out, do you think you were frozen, like in a coma perhaps?

Noah: No, that couldn't be right because I must have done something during that lapse of time seeing as my girlfriend was obviously upset by it.

Therapist: I have a theory. Want to hear it?

Noah: Not really, but go ahead.

Therapist: Are you sure? [*Noah nods.*] Maybe another part of you took over the body and said or did something to your girlfriend.

Noah: Another part?

Therapist: Yeah. It would still be you, but a different part of you, like an angry part, or a protector, perhaps even a separate identity.

Noah: Do you think I'm crazy?

Therapist: No, I don't think you are crazy. I think you learned to dissociate as a way to cope with difficult situations in childhood. I like to think of it as a survival technique that you figured out on your own.

Noah: You think that's what I got? A split personality?

Therapist: We used to call it multiple personality disorder, but now we call it dissociative identity disorder or DID. Yes, I think it's possible that you have this.

Noah: I'm not sure I like where you are going with this. I told you I didn't want to go into all those memories. I've put it all behind me.

Therapist: I totally respect that, and I'm not asking you to talk about those memories now. The only reason I brought it up is to explain how other identities could have been formed in childhood.

Noah: I don't understand.

Therapist: It is a way to survive really bad things as a child. When you were little, you might have created a new identity who doesn't remember the event. That new part can take over and go play or go to school without worries because the new part doesn't remember what happened.

Noah: If I did all that, why wouldn't I remember it now?

Therapist: That's the thing. There may be an identity hidden inside who does remember it. That part might feel angry, sad, or needy.

Noah: [*He pauses.*] Are you saying another identity took over and did something to my girlfriend?

Therapist: It's possible. What do you think?

Noah: My girlfriend does tell me that sometimes I act like a different person, but I thought she was just exaggerating.

There are many different directions this conversation can go from here. It may take many such conversations before the therapist is able to make a definitive diagnosis of DID and the client is able to accept the diagnosis. One important thing about psychoeducation is that it works best when it is integrated into therapeutic conversation that is relevant to the current topic. For example, some clients will express a special interest in learning more about how DID develops, including brain processes. When this occurs, you can share more information and also refer the client to other resources they can study. Other clients are disinterested in such details, and little tidbits of psychoeducation offered here and there may be all that's needed.

Sometimes, the client may ask you to share more psychoeducation with their spouse, partner, family member, religious leader, or friend. Once a client has accepted their diagnosis, helping their support team understand the diagnosis can be enormously helpful. This can mitigate the understandable confusion and fear that individuals often experience when they learn that their loved one has a DID diagnosis. As therapy progresses, the client is likely to begin to make changes in their behavior, and if those who care about them understand DID, they will be able to offer support more easily.

As the client improves, psychoeducation does not fall away. Rather, it often becomes more detailed as the client moves forward in understanding themselves and their system. If you are willing to keep an open mind, continue to learn from the literature, and seek out further training, you will be able to offer additional psychoeducation when needed. You would also benefit by listening closely to your clients with DID, as you will learn much about the process since every person with DID is unique.

BRAIN FUNCTIONING

When clients become curious about how the brain functions, it is important that you honor their request with accurate information. This means you need to continue to educate yourself on this topic, as breakthroughs in brain research frequently occur. One place to start is to borrow a metaphor from Bessel van der Kolk (2014), who compares three key parts of the brain to household objects or actions: the thalamus is the cook, the amygdala is the smoke detector, and the prefrontal cortex is the watchtower.

The thalamus is the part of the brain that processes sensory information from all five senses, so you can think of it as a cook. It blends all the information together and quickly sends it to the amygdala, which functions like a smoke detector because it screeches a warning whenever it thinks this incoming sensory information indicates danger. The cook also sends this same sensory information to the prefrontal cortex, which functions as a watchtower in that it examines the person's surroundings to determine whether the threat is real or not. Because it takes longer for information to reach the watchtower, the smoke alarm sometimes starts screeching before the watchtower even gets the signal. If the watchtower decides there is no threat, it sends a message back to the smoke detector to stop its warning. Though this seems like a complicated process, it actually happens over the course of a few seconds.

Among highly functioning individuals, the smoke alarm will generally only go off when there is indeed a threat, and when it makes a mistake, the watchtower is quick to turn it off. However, for clients with complex trauma, things don't go as planned. The smoke detector is oversensitive and issues warnings when there is no threat, much like what happens if you install a smoke detector too close to the stove. In addition, a heavy dose of anxiety can result in the watchtower being less able to quickly determine if a particular situation is safe. All the while, the smoke detector continues to screech, which activates the fight, flight, freeze response. Over time, chronic activation of this response can result in long-term stress and have toxic effects on the body.

The following dialogue is an example of how you might share this neuroscience information with a client who has accepted and is comfortable with their diagnosis of DID. In this scenario, the primary alter is a responsible adult named Patricia, and there is also a male protector alter named Pat:

Patricia: I just don't understand why I keep yelling at my children. I try hard to stop myself, but I keep doing it.

Therapist: Do you ever lose time during these interactions with your children? [*The therapist is interested in the amount of amnesia that the client experiences, consistent with the goal of getting to know the alters, the second pillar.*]

Patricia: I used to before I started therapy with you, but it is rare now. Pat seems to be content staying in the background. It's me doing the yelling. I remember every detail. Sometimes I wish I didn't, because I feel so guilty afterward.

Therapist: Is Pat aware of your struggle with this? [*The therapist is now focusing on the three Cs, the third pillar.*]

Patricia: [*She pauses and closes her eyes.*] He is adamant. He wants to stay out of it. I think he's pushing me to solve it myself.

Therapist: Okay. That's fine. The reason I asked was to see if he might be able to help you with it. [*The therapist is gently suggesting one of the three Cs—cooperation.*]

Patricia: He won't. I just want to understand why I can't stop.

Therapist: Do you remember when we talked about the activation process and the fight, flight, freeze response?

Patricia: Vaguely, but I'm not sure how it would relate to my situation.

Therapist: I just think our kiddos know how to push our buttons. I'd be surprised if this didn't happen to you now and then.

Patricia: But that's no excuse for yelling at them.

Therapist: I totally agree. I'm just wondering if it would help you to understand in more detail how our brains work when we get activated. Then we could talk about ways to deal differently with it.

Patricia: Yeah, okay.

Therapist: To start, could you describe a recent situation where you yelled at your children and felt guilty afterward? [*In order for psychoeducation to be helpful, it needs to be connected to real-life events.*]

Patricia: Okay. Just this morning, Kayla, my littlest one, refused to put her shoes on and we only had a few minutes before the bus would arrive. Ben and Lilly were dressed, standing by the door and ready to go.

Therapist: What happened next?

Patricia: I stayed calm and told her it was time to go. She just sat on the couch and wouldn't look at me. I told her to put her shoes on right now. She didn't budge, so I grabbed her shoes and started to put them on her. She pulled away. That's when I yelled.

Therapist: How are you feeling right now, talking about this? [*The therapist is checking to see how activated Patricia is, so as to decide whether to suggest some resourcing—the first pillar—or whether to have her continue with the story.*]

Patricia: No, I'm okay.

Therapist: Can you check in with your body? What number are you at right now?

For the purposes of this scenario, let's assume the therapist and Patricia have worked extensively in the past on using a subjective unit of distress (SUD)* rating scale to monitor her activation level on a scale from 0 to 10, so Patricia understands what the therapist is asking. When clients can evaluate their internal state and provide a SUD number, they are in fact doing a little bit of resourcing.

Patricia: I'm at a 4, but as you know, I never go below a 3, so I'm fine.

Therapist: Sounds good. Let's just take a breath together to be sure. [*The therapist is offering one more bit of resourcing.*] Now, can you remember what your number was when you first approached Kayla? You said you were calm.

Patricia: I was probably a 5, because I was worried the kids would miss the bus and I'd be late to work if I had to drive them to school.

Therapist: So, you were under a lot of pressure at that moment.

Patricia: Seems like that's how it is every morning.

Therapist: Okay. Let's slow it down a bit. You told her it was time to go, and she wouldn't look at you. What was your number then? [*Slowing down the process in describing events is an excellent way for the client to remember new details.*]

Patricia: Probably rising. A 6 or 7.

Therapist: Then you told her to put her shoes on. Is that right?

Patricia: She crossed her arms and pouted. The little snot. So I grabbed her shoes and tried to put them on her, but she pulled back. Then I yelled.

Therapist: What was your activation level then?

Patricia: At least an 8, maybe a 9. After I yelled, she gave in and let me put her shoes on.

* The SUD scale, which was developed by Joseph Wolpe in 1969, was originally a scale from 0 to 100, then later changed to 0 to 10, with higher numbers indicating higher levels of distress.

Therapist: Did all your children end up catching the bus?

Patricia: Barely.

It is good practice when discussing emotionally distraught events or memories of trauma to continue the conversation, if possible, beyond the moment of intensity. In this example, there was a resolution: the children caught the bus. By discussing the resolution, the client crosses an event boundary (Ranganath, 2024), and the memory tends to lose some of its emotional intensity.

Therapist: Did you calm yourself down after that?

Patricia: I had to because I had to rush off to work.

Therapist: Okay, we'll get back to that later. Now that I have an idea of what happened, I can tell you more about what was probably going on in your brain through these events, if you think that would help.

Patricia: Go for it.

This is a moment for the therapist, who may be excited about sharing their considerable insights and understandings about brain functioning, to listen closely to Patricia, including not only her words but also her tone of voice and body language. Clients often want to please the therapist, and if the therapist picks up that Patricia isn't really interested in further discussion of brain functioning, then the therapist needs to back away from the psychoeducation process and refocus on what Patricia wants to explore. For the purposes of this example, Patricia is interested in further discussion about the brain.

Therapist: Okay, there is a part of your brain called the thalamus, but we're going to call it the cook.

Patricia: Why the cook?

Therapist: We call it the cook because it is the part of the brain that is constantly getting information from your senses: what you see, what you hear, what you smell, what you taste, and what you feel. Its job is to mix together the mismatch of data and cook it into a soup.

Patricia: Sounds weird, but go on.

Therapist: It takes that soup and sends it in two directions: very quickly to the back of the brain, and a little more slowly to the front of the brain.

Patricia: Okay, so in my situation, what is in the soup?

Therapist: What do you think might have been in the soup on the morning we are discussing?

Patricia: When I think of it now, I remember the image of Kayla crossing her arms and pouting. It made me so mad. If I'd have done something like that when I was her age—

Therapist: What would have happened?

Patricia: I wouldn't have been able to sit down for a week.

Therapist: Ah, do you want to take a minute to come to terms with that memory?

Patricia: No, it's okay. It's in the past. I would never hurt Kayla like that.

At this point, the therapist may decide to step away from the psychoeducation discussion to assist Patricia in handling this emerging memory. Since she has a diagnosis of DID, it could also be an opportunity to do some more work with inner communication—the third pillar. For the purposes of this scenario, we will continue with the psychoeducation discussion.

Therapist: Okay, so you've provided an excellent example of how powerful images, when included in the soup, can affect the outcome. In your example, the cook would include this image of Kayla crossing her arms and pouting as one ingredient in the soup, along with other ingredients. The cook might also include your desire to get going. There might be your worry of getting in trouble at work. There might be a picture of Ben and Lilly being good and contrasting that with Kayla being naughty. The cook, however, doesn't make any judgments about the data. It just organizes it into a soup and sends it on its way.

Patricia: Okay, what happens next?

Therapist: In the back part of the brain, which is the most primitive part of the brain, is a structure called the amygdala. But we are going to call it the smoke detector. [*Patricia looks interested.*] The smoke detector gets the soup and has to decide whether to start screeching based on the ingredients in it. If it senses you are in danger, or even if you *might* be in danger, it will screech.

Patricia: Why would it think I was in danger? There's no way little Kayla is going to hurt me.

Therapist: It's possible it could have pulled up one of your memories associated with feeling threatened.

Patricia: Like what?

Therapist: I can't say for sure, but I do remember you once told me there was no way you were ever able to say no to an adult. What if your brain mistook Kayla's situation with the fear you had when you were a child?

Patricia: My brain could do that?

Therapist: Yeah. The brain is truly amazing.

Patricia: I see what you are getting at. This would make the smoke detector start screeching.

Therapist: Absolutely right. Do you have a smoke detector in your apartment?

Patricia: I've got two: one in my bedroom and one in the hallway.

Therapist: Has it ever gone off when there was no danger, no fire, and no smoke?

Patricia: The one in the hallway used to be near the kitchen. It was going off all the time whenever too much steam would come off a pot that was boiling, so that's why I had to move it to the hallway.

Therapist: And when it did go off, when there was in fact no fire, what did you do?

Patricia: I had to push the little button so it would stop screeching.

Therapist: The other really important factor is that people who have early childhood trauma, like yourself, end up with an oversensitive smoke detector. Even a hint of the fear you experienced as a child could be enough to set it off.

Patricia: Okay, go on. What happens next?

Therapist: The cook not only sends the information to the smoke detector at the back of the brain, but it also sends it to the prefrontal cortex at the front of the brain. We'll call that the watchtower.

Patricia: Why the watchtower?

Therapist: Because it has the ability to look around and make an informed decision as to whether there really is a threat.

Patricia: In this example, what would the watchtower see?

Therapist: My guess is it sees Kayla and realizes she is upset and obstinate. If the watchtower is functioning at its best, it will also notice that she is no real threat to your safety, and it will immediately send a signal back to the smoke detector to stop its screeching. Once it does that, it is much easier for you to calm down and find a way to deal with the situation without yelling at your daughter.

Patricia: And if it isn't functioning at its best?

Therapist: What do you think would happen?

Patricia: I would lose it and regret it afterward.

Therapist: You got it.

Patricia: Are you telling me my watchtower is broken? And I know for a fact that I have lots of bad memories that might influence the smoke detector. And it sounds like my smoke detector needs a major repair or replacement as well. This isn't exactly making me feel better.

Therapist: Maybe it's because I haven't got to the good part yet.

Patricia: [*She smiles.*] Then get to it—and quick.

Therapist: Now that we have an idea what isn't working, we can figure out why, and fix it.

Patricia: I'm waiting.

Therapist: Okay. The breathing exercises and mindfulness techniques you've been doing are key in this process.

Patricia: You'll have to explain that a bit more.

Therapist: You will still get activated from time to time, and probably more often than folks who don't have an oversensitive smoke detector. But by practicing breathing exercises and other forms of resourcing, you are in fact relaxing the body, which will, in time, teach the smoke detector to stop overreacting.

Patricia: And how about the mindfulness? I'm still not very good at that.

Therapist: With mindfulness, the tiniest bit of success can have a big effect. That's because it improves the watchtower's awareness of the environment so it can determine false alarms more quickly and efficiently. This also helps the cook adjust the ingredients of the soup.

Patricia: And how about the bad memories?

Therapist: This is more complicated. Remember when we talked about body memories?

Patricia: Yeah.

Therapist: Sometimes uncomfortable bodily reactions are caused by fragmented pieces of traumatic memories that weren't stored efficiently when the event occurred. This can cause the smoke detector to go off when one of these memories resurfaces. Remember that the smoke detector's job is to do whatever is necessary for you to survive. It would much prefer to cause a false alarm than to miss an actual threat. Its default position is to shriek. Any perceived threat is judged guilty until proven innocent.

Patricia: So, how do we fix it?

Therapist: Actually, there are several ways. You remember the three Cs we discussed earlier?

Patricia: Communication and co-consciousness. I forgot the third one.

Therapist: Cooperation. Sometimes that one is the most difficult. The barriers between the alters keep some of your memories walled off.

Patricia: Yeah, there is lots I don't remember from my childhood.

Therapist: As you get better with the three Cs, some of those barriers will slowly start to weaken.

Patricia: That sounds a little scary to me.

Therapist: We will always go at your own pace. As we discussed earlier, if we are ever discussing something that is too much for you, you can just let me know and we will slow it down or stop talking about it all together, until you are ready.

Patricia: Okay.

Therapist: There are also ways we can work together in therapy to reprocess some of those memories to reduce their ability to affect you on a day-to-day basis. Does any of this make sense to you? Does it fit with your experience? [*Patricia closes her eyes for a brief moment.*]

Pat: [*He opens his eyes and looks down at the floor.*] You don't understand.

Therapist: Is that still you, Patricia?

Pat: You don't recognize me?

Therapist: Pat?

Pat: Bingo.

Therapist: I'm happy to get a chance to talk with you, Pat. Have you've been listening?

Pat: Of course. That's part of my job. Don't you know?

Therapist: What do you think of what we talked about? [*Due to the emergence of Pat, new opportunities to get to know the alters have become available—the second pillar.*]

Pat: Sounds like a lot of mumbo jumbo to me.

Therapist: Do you remember the incident we were talking about?

Pat: Patricia lets Kayla get away with too much. I'm glad she yelled at her. It's the only way she ever gets Kayla to listen and do what she is told.

Therapist: Okay. I hear what you are saying. I'm also interested in what you think about my conversation with Patricia regarding the memories.

Pat: I think it's best to let sleeping dogs lie.

Therapist: I'd like to keep in touch with you about this as things progress in therapy. How are you feeling these days about Patricia coming in to see me? I know you had misgivings originally.

Pat: It's okay for now. I have to admit she seems happier, but I will reserve judgment.

Therapist: I understand your reluctance, and I appreciate your input as we proceed.

Depending on how much time is left in the session, the therapist might attempt to get Patricia's input back into the conversation, either by having Pat check in with her, or by having Patricia come back out to respond to Pat's concerns. At any rate, the focus will return to the three Cs.

CHAPTER 9

THE OUTER WORLD

When engaging in therapy with clients with DID, large amounts of time and energy will be spent focusing on their inner worlds, where complex interactions among alters occur. As dissociative barriers gradually break down, opportunities for traumatic healing emerge. However, changes that occur in the outside world will also, by necessity, affect the inner world. After all, clients live their lives in the outside world, and consequences, whether positive or negative, have to be handled in that outside world. Therefore, you must seek out a balance between maintaining an inner focus versus an outer focus. In this chapter, I explore the many realities and stressors that clients face in their interactions with the physical outside world.

ACCOMMODATIONS

When working with any client, it is essential that you cultivate a therapeutic environment characterized by the principles of trauma-informed care (Wilson et al., 2013), but this is even more important when working with clients with DID. To maintain a trauma-informed stance, your policies and procedures must acknowledge and account for the effects of trauma on the behavior and attitudes that clients may present with. This is not to suggest that clients are not expected to take responsibility for their actions, especially when such actions cause stress or harm to others. It does mean, though, that you must apply careful clinical judgment with regard to how strictly or loosely you decide to interpret your policies and procedures.

One salient example is no-show policies. No-shows and cancellations are costly to therapeutic businesses, and many agencies and private practice clinics have attempted to manage this financial drain by creating strict policies. For example, if clients exceed a certain number of no-shows or cancellations without a twenty-four-hour notice, the business may terminate therapy with these clients. Others charge a fee for such no-shows. Still others require those with too many no-shows to prove their motivation before returning to therapy by attending a no-show group or some other punitive process. To avoid this, some agencies use a proactive approach of using reminder calls or texts as a way to reduce the incidents. In my decades of work as a therapist in both private practice and mental health centers, I have never seen the result of any of these efforts to be totally effective. There will always be some cancellations and no-shows.

Therefore, clinical judgment must be a factor in setting and enforcing these policies. For example, no matter how strictly an agency decides to enforce its no-show policy that cancellations must be made twenty-four hours in advance, they would not penalize a client for a no-show if the client had a medical emergency on their way to their appointment. As a more pertinent example, let's say a therapist has a relatively new client whom they've diagnosed with DID, and the client no-shows for their appointment. In discussing this later with the client, the therapist discovers that the client missed the appointment because an alter who didn't know there was an appointment took over fronting the body, and the primary didn't retake control until the next day. In such a case, a strict enforcement of the no-show policy wouldn't make any therapeutic sense. Instead, the therapist might create a new therapy goal of helping the primary alter develop enough agency to prevent such an occurrence in the future, as well as setting up some inner communication and cooperation so that the newly emerging alter can get their needs met in another way.

SAFETY ISSUES

In addition to accommodations, safety issues must take on a high priority in working with clients with DID. Even as adults, many of these individuals live in situations where they face abuse or the potential of abuse, struggle with suicidality, or are at risk of engaging in risky behaviors due to amnesia caused by the switching of alters. In the next sections, I examine each of these safety issues in greater depth.

Ongoing Abuse

It is not uncommon for clients with DID to experience ongoing abuse from a partner or a previous perpetrator and not reveal this to you, especially at the beginning of treatment. One possible reason for this is that the alters who interact with you have no knowledge of these events. Another possibility is they are aware of the experiences, but the perpetrator has threatened them or someone they care about if they reveal it. Still another possibility is that internal alters justify the abuse and have forbidden the primary to reveal it. Since it may be impossible to know whether a client is being abused, the best practice is to keep this possibility in mind while proceeding with the three pillars with the hope that eventually, you can create enough trust in the therapeutic relationship whereby the client will reveal what is happening. Then you can address it.

Suicide Risk

Another prominent safety concern that can emerge among clients with DID is suicide risk, as over 70 percent of outpatients with DID have attempted suicide, with many having made multiple attempts (APA, 2022). As a result, safety planning becomes especially important. Aspiration 2 is relevant here: "Remind yourself that your client is the whole system, not any particular alter." It is unlikely that every alter in the system is suicidal. If this were the case, they would have already completed suicide. Rather, there will be one or more suicidal alters, as well as one or more alters who oppose suicide and want to live. In addition, there may be other alters who are ambivalent or are so disengaged that they have no opinion.

By utilizing the three Cs, you can identify those alters who wish to die and those who wish to live. Once you identify them, you can explore the values and reasons behind each alter. Often, the suicidal alters have specific reasons for their position. They may, for example, be stuck in the past and believe they are still in danger of being abused, in which case they view suicide as more preferable to enduring one more day of such abuse. In this case, reeducation is paramount. You will want to help the responsible adult alters reeducate these suicidal alters, who are usually little ones, that they are all grown up and safe. Some suicidal alters are unaware that if the body dies, all the other alters will die along with it. Convincing them of this fact is sometimes sufficient for them to abandon their suicidal plans, as they do not want to harm the others in the system. This reeducation process may take some time, so one strategy would be to negotiate with the suicidal alters and get them to agree to postpone their actions until more of the reeducation can take place. When this is not possible, creating a safety plan involving commitments from the alters who are against suicide can be effective.

The key to remember is that if you are only talking to the particular alter who is fronting the body at the time, any attempt to do safety planning is unlikely to be successful. If a client is psychiatrically hospitalized due to a suicide threat or attempt, you will ideally want to have this conversation with all relevant alters prior to the client's discharge. Since it can be difficult, if not impossible, to gain access to the client during their hospitalization, I recommend having the client sign a release beforehand giving you permission to consult with the psychiatrist who is taking care of the patient during their hospitalization. Otherwise, once the client is discharged, this would be an important conversation to have during their first outpatient session.

Homicide Risk

It is common in the media to portray clients with DID as potentially homicidal. An evil personality emerges and kills someone, goes back inside, and leaves the "host personality" to deal with the consequences, without any recollection of the deed. I have certainly worked with clients with DID who have had homicidal alters, so I am not denying this scenario could happen, but it is the exception rather than the norm. In my experience, when clients do have homicidal alters, they are often rageful child or adolescent alters who wish to exact revenge on their perpetrators. It is likely that those alters have been either locked away somewhere in the internal world or pushed down to a different layer where they have no access to the outside world. However, this doesn't eliminate the risk. When you learn about such alters, much can be done in enlisting other alters to slowly reeducate them in a similar way to working with suicidal alters.

Risky Behavior

Due to early childhood traumatic experiences, there will probably be alters who remember the abuse and who wish to seek revenge against the abusers. Other alters, as I discussed in chapter 7, may be prone to engage in risky behaviors like alcohol or drug use, which is likely to result in retraumatization. Some alters may even wish to harm the body. In all these situations, the three pillars will be useful in interrupting the tendencies of alters who are prone to risky behaviors. For example, angry alters can learn resourcing techniques to quiet their dysregulation. Alters wishing to self-harm can be watched over by other alters until they accept other roles they might play in the system. Revengeful alters can be informed of the negative consequences that violence would have on the whole system. Alters seeking adventure and stimulation can find safer ways to meet their needs. Child alters wishing to run amok can be watched over, nurtured, and reparented by other alters.

Since many, if not most, clients with DID have experienced sexual trauma, risky sexual expression is frequently problematic as well. As with other complex childhood trauma survivors, dissociation is common during sexual activity. There may be sexualized alters (sometimes children or adolescents) who emerge to actively participate during sex. Unethical sexual partners may consciously or unconsciously call out these alters because they are often more flirtatious and engaging than the adult alters. This is problematic, as the sexualized alters end up reenacting sexual abuse scenarios to the detriment of the whole system.

As therapy progresses and you learn more about the client's inner world and the roles played by various alters, gentle inquiries about the client's sexual activity can be helpful in determining whether risky sexual behavior is happening. As with other issues, you should be wise enough to not offer solutions, but you can be a positive influence in facilitating some problem-solving among the alters. If it is safe and there is informed consent from all the known alters, you can offer to bring the client's partner in for a session, should the client wish to share their concerns in hopes of finding a resolution.

BUILDING A SUPPORT SYSTEM

There are great differences among clients with DID in terms of their social skills and their ability to create a support system for themselves. Some clients already have what they need in terms of a spouse, a family, work acquaintances, and friends. In these situations, you need to accomplish very little in the therapy setting when it comes to establishing social support, although conversations about whether or not a client should reveal their multiplicity, and to whom, can be useful.

More often than not, though, clients with DID tend to be either isolated or caught up with others who are less than supportive. Some clients are so isolated that the only people they feel they can trust are the professionals in their lives, in which case you can end up being the totality of their support system. This is not sustainable in the long term, but it may be the reality in the initial stages of the therapeutic process. From there, you can attempt to add other professionals to the client's support network, such as their primary care physician or psychiatric provider. Some mental health centers also have community support persons whose job is to help clients handle day-to-day problems, such as dealing with insurance, filing disability claims, and assessing other community resources (e.g., food banks and government assistance) for those who are living in poverty. For clients who are religious, it can help to reach out to a trusted pastor or a peer in their church. For those who have struggled with an addiction, Alcoholics Anonymous and Narcotics Anonymous groups can sometimes serve this purpose. Other twelve-step groups may also be helpful, such as Emotions Anonymous.

Because many clients with DID have had past negative experiences with professionals (e.g., a therapist who didn't believe the client when they shared their experience), it is not surprising that many clients are hesitant to reveal their condition to their providers. In an ideal situation, a therapist is part of a multidisciplinary team of professionals, all of whom have a good understanding and acceptance of DID. In many cases, however, this is not the case. Many therapists who work with clients with DID struggle to find DID-friendly professionals with whom to collaborate.

As a result, there may be times when a client asks you to intervene for them in communicating with another professional. It is preferable if the client is empowered to engage with this provider on their own, but there are certainly instances where the client's request can be granted. For example, if the only available psychiatric or medical provider is not well-versed in dissociation, it would be more effective for you to speak to that provider, professional to professional. Besides having the client sign a release, it would be important to check in with all known alters to explain the situation and get informed consent (see chapter 10).

Overall, the search for supportive and trustworthy people is often a long process for clients with DID, but it's certainly worth the effort. Besides providing enjoyment and the pleasure of human contact, a vibrant support system can provide needed reinforcement in times of crisis. It also provides clients with an opportunity to practice two of the three Cs—inner communication and cooperation—in the outside world. As the client develops the communication and cooperation skills needed to interact with the alters in their internal world, they will hopefully be able to generalize some of those skills to supportive others in the outside world.

MANAGING CRISES

An issue that comes up frequently when working with complex trauma is the frequent crises that clients face in their lives. It would be unethical to ignore or diminish the suffering involved in these day-to-day crises. At the same time, problem-solving techniques, no matter how sophisticated, will be unlikely to create positive outcomes if the particular problem they work on changes every week. Not only does it make it difficult to work together toward a cohesive goal, but it can lead you to experience frustration that compromises the therapeutic relationship. When this occurs, integrating the three pillars (resourcing, getting to know the alters, and the three Cs) into therapeutic conversations regarding crisis situations resolves many of these dilemmas. The following dialogue describes how this might look in practice.

Imagine Emma comes to a session in an activated state and is eager to discuss her recent conflict with her sister. Here is how the conversation begins:

Emma: My sister is mad at me—really mad. I tried to be nice to her, but now I'm getting pretty angry myself.

Therapist: Okay, Emma. Can you tell me more? [*The therapist is genuinely curious and is skilled at active nonjudgmental listening.*]

Emma: I posted a photo on my Facebook page, and she didn't like it. [*She pauses and shifts in her seat.*]

Therapist: Would you be willing to share with me was the picture was?

Emma: I'd rather not.

Therapist: That's okay. You don't have to. Do you know why the photo was upsetting to your sister?

Emma: She claims I broke confidence with her—that she didn't want me to tell anyone about it.

Therapist: I see. And what is your view of it?

Emma: She never said to keep it a secret. [*Her demeaner shifts from anger to sadness.*]

Therapist: I notice something has shifted in you. Can you say more about it?

Emma: I'm confused. She's so critical of me all the time. I can never seem to do the right thing.

So far, similar conversations as this could easily occur with any client, whether they have DID or not. There are a number of ways the therapist can continue in this situation, depending on the therapist-client relationship, the therapist's skill set, and whatever past issues the therapist and Emma have worked on together. For example, the therapist might do some problem-solving with Emma, helping her see if she wants to repair the conflict with her sister and, if so, how she might proceed.

Another approach might be to examine Emma's tendency to put herself down and brainstorm ways she might counteract those negative practices. The therapist could also ask historical questions regarding Emma's previous relationship with her sister or explore Emma's value system regarding how she views family relationships. There are many other possibilities, all of which may or may not be helpful to the client, and none of which would be wrong. Various modalities may be helpful in pursuing these conversations, including CBT, DBT, acceptance and commitment therapy (ACT), or narrative therapy. No matter the approach, if the client has a habit of bringing in a different crisis each week and has a difficulty following through with any suggestions or ideas that are discussed, this new crisis could create some frustration or impatience within the therapist.

However, if a client is diagnosed with DID, a whole different kind of conversation is possible when you embrace the three pillars. Here is one example of how the session could move ahead.

Therapist: Let's take a breath together. [*This is the therapist's attempt to bring in the first pillar, resourcing.*]

Emma: [*Emma is the primary.*] Not right now. I'm too upset.

Therapist: That's fine. I'm assuming I am talking to Emma right now. Is that the case?

Emma: Duh.

Therapist: Do you actually remember posting the photo on your Facebook page? [*This question opens the door to the possibility that some other alter may have been involved in the event. This is probably not a question a therapist would ask a client who didn't suffer from dissociation.*]

Emma: Sort of, yeah. [*When clients are ambivalent about their involvement in an event, this is a good indicator that some dissociation was occurring at the time.*]

Therapist: Can you remember what you were thinking or feeling when you posted it?

Emma: [*She pauses.*] Not really, maybe I was on autopilot.

Therapist: Is it possible there was another alter who was involved? [*Here, the therapist is introducing the second pillar, getting to know the alters.*]

Emma: I don't know. I doubt it.

Therapist: Would you be willing right now, to close your eyes, check inside, and ask if anyone else was involved or has any information about what happened when you posted the photo?

Emma: [*She takes a deep breath, closes her eyes, and pauses.*]

Even though Emma refused to engage in any formal resourcing, the therapist knows Emma can rely on their attunement as a form of resourcing. Alternately, the therapist could use a SUD scale to have Emma describe how upset she is. If her number is above 5, the therapist might want to try other methods of resourcing to get her activation level down to a safer level. This, however, would depend on the therapist's clinical judgment and how well they know Emma, as some clients identify as a 5 at baseline and are quite capable of handling stressful events at a 6 or 7. Other clients might get overwhelmed at a 5.

Emma: No one will answer. I can tell that Jacob is upset though.

Therapist: How can you tell Jacob is upset?

Emma: My stomach hurts, and I'm starting to get a headache.

Therapist: Is this how Jacob communicates with you sometimes? [*The therapist is now immersed in an exploration of inner communication, one of the three Cs.*]

Client: I've never thought about it that way, but yeah, it could be.

Therapist: Now that you are aware of that, would you be willing to address Jacob directly and ask him about the Facebook photo?

Emma: [*She closes her eyes again, and the expression on her face shifts.*]

Therapist: Is Jacob talking to you now, or does he want to come out and talk to me directly?

At this point, Jacob might pop out, but if not, Emma may still have some important information from Jacob about how he feels about the sister and his motivation to post the photo. Maybe Jacob wanted to hurt the sister because he remembers a time when the sister was mean to him. Maybe he was trying get Emma's attention. Another possibility is that Emma opens her eyes and says that Jacob won't reveal his secrets. Regardless how the conversation proceeds, several things have already been accomplished:

1. The therapist is no longer in a position of having to provide suggestions or ideas to Emma as to how to deal with her conflict with her sister. This can be a massive relief and reduces the risk of countertransference and burnout.
2. No matter Emma's response, from a total denial of any inner communication to one of maximum cooperation, the importance of the three Cs has been emphasized, along with planting the seeds for resourcing, and some steps have also been made in the goal of getting to know the alters. All three pillars are now in play.
3. If the therapist has been frustrated with Emma's lack of follow-up in the past, this becomes much less of an issue. Rather than hoping Emma will follow through with whatever plan she and the therapist have devised to deal with the sister, the problem has now shifted to an internal problem.

Let's imagine that Emma was unable to glean any information from Jacob as the conversation continues.

Emma: I tried to talk to Jacob, but nothing happened. My stomach doesn't hurt anymore, but my headache is getting worse.

Therapist: Would you be willing to take a couple simple breaths with me now? [*The therapist gently reintroduces the first pillar, resourcing.*]

Emma: I can try, but I doubt it will do any good.

There is still evidence that Emma is activated since her headache is getting worse, but she no longer has the anger and sadness she had at the beginning of the session when thinking about her sister. Due to this change, she is now willing to attempt the breathing resource that the therapist has suggested.

Therapist: You don't have to follow any fancy breathing technique. Just breathe normally, but allow yourself to be aware of the breath. [*They take several breaths together.*]

Emma: Something is happening. [*She shifts slightly in the chair.*]

Jacob: [*He speaks in a deeper voice.*] What do you want?

Through this conversation, the therapist realizes that one possible reason Emma was reluctant earlier to do resource breathing is that it relaxes the body and makes it easier for internal alters to take over. Knowing this, the therapist refrains from suggesting to Emma that she practice breathing on her own. Later in therapy, if Emma, as the responsible adult in the system, develops effective ways of monitoring the switching process, it will be safer to focus on breathing as a primary resource technique.

Therapist: Hello there. Who am I talking to?

Jacob: [*He looks around the room, expressionless.*] That's not important, just tell me what you want. [*It is common for some alters to initially be reluctant to share information, especially their name. This is especially prevalent with protectors. Child alters, on the other hand, are often quite open with sharing things.*]

Therapist: I was wondering if you were listening in as I was talking to Emma.

Jacob: What if I was?

Therapist: I hope you were. [*This simple comment is a way to acknowledge the value of co-consciousness.*] Did you know that Emma has been having some conflicts with her sister?

Jacob: Her sister is a bitch.

Therapist: I appreciate you sharing your thoughts about this. Do you know if Emma is nearby and able to listen in to our conversation?

This last question keeps the therapist focused on advocating co-consciousness. Alternatively, the therapist could have asked a question designed to get to know this new alter better. For example, the therapist may have said, "I appreciate you letting me know how you feel about Emma's sister. Have you had much direct contact with her?" This of course, would have led the conversation in a different, but also potentially helpful, direction.

Jacob: No, she left.

Therapist: Do you know where she went?

Jacob: Why are you asking me all these questions? I can hardly keep track of her and all the others. [*Although the therapist chooses not to pursue this* *thought, they note to themself the importance of this new information: this alter has taken on the important role of managing the other alters inside.*]

Therapist: I didn't mean to stress you out. I will back off from all the questions. As you may know, I have been working with Emma for some time now, and I have been encouraging her to get to know the others inside. If you would like to share your perspective on this, I would be happy to listen.

Jacob: I have to go now. [*He closes his eyes.*]

Therapist: Okay. Thanks for coming out to meet me. Can you make way for Emma to come back out?

Emma: [*She opens her eyes.*] It's me.

Therapist: Emma?

Emma: [*She places her hand on her forehead.*] My headache is worse. [*It is common for clients with DID to experience headaches when they switch identities, especially if it happens quickly and without planning.*]

Therapist: Emma, I'm glad you're back. Were you able to listen in to my conversation while you were gone?

Emma: I heard parts of it.

Therapist: I'm happy to hear that. Do you happen to know if it was Jacob I was talking to, or someone else?

Emma: [*She pauses and closes her eyes briefly, then opens them again.*] It's weird, but I just heard Jacob say something.

Therapist: Can you share what he said?

Emma: I won't repeat it. It was kind of rude.

Therapist: Sounds like it was him, then?

Emma: Definitely.

Therapist: I was wondering what it was like for you to hear directly from Jacob just now? [*The therapist is acknowledging the improvement in inner communication while also seeking more information.*]

Emma: Kind of weird actually. I don't really like him very much. He likes to curse and I don't believe in that.

Therapist: Okay, I understand what you are saying. I am encouraged though that you now have some communication with him. Maybe in time you could learn to work together. [*The therapist is introducing cooperation, the second component of the three Cs.*] It doesn't appear he is going anywhere soon.

Emma: [*She laughs softly.*] Are you saying I am stuck with him?

Therapist: I guess I would say you are in this together.

Despite the seriousness of the work, Emma's smiles and laughter suggest two things. First, it points to the strength of the attunement between Emma and her therapist, and second, it is a testament to Emma's intelligence and resiliency.

Therapist: We have a few minutes left, and we didn't really talk much about your conflict with your sister. That's on me. I kept asking you questions about Jacob and focused more on your communication with him rather than your communication with your sister. [*The therapist is acknowledging that they have privileged a discussion about the inner world over a discussion about Emma's conflict with her sister.*] What has that been like for you?

Emma: Well, nothing has been resolved, that's for sure.

Therapist: Would you like to know why I asked those questions? [*Emma nods.*] My thought was that if Jacob or another alter from inside has been involved in some way with your conflict with your sister, any steps you might take alone to resolve it probably wouldn't work.

Emma: [*She pauses for a moment, appearing to be thinking or checking inside.*] It's okay.

Therapist: Were you just talking to someone inside? [*The therapist is pushing the importance of communication with this question, which could be a mistake, depending on how strong the therapist-client relationship is.*]

Emma: You sure are nosey today.

Therapist: Thanks for letting me know how you feel about my question. I apologize if I was pushing too hard. I think I got a little excited about how you seem to be developing better inner communication.

Note that the therapist is engaging in self-disclosure with this comment. In this situation, it serves the therapeutic relationship. The client has expressed concerns about the therapist being "nosey." The therapist apologizes for pushing too hard, which is a way to emphasize aspiration 3: "Center the client system in therapy rather than centering yourself as the expert." It acknowledges Emma's right to object, and it reiterates that it is the therapist's responsibility to back off when she asks.

In addition, this comment provides an honest explanation for the therapist's emotional response and the therapist's motivation in asking the question. This relates directly to aspiration 5: "Be congruent in your presentation with courageous honesty and transparency." Clients, especially those with early childhood trauma, tend to be very good at perceiving incongruence. When the therapist disclosed how their excitement influenced their questioning, Emma was able to perceive their congruence, in turn enhancing trust and attunement.

Emma: It's alright. The fact is, I'm not sure what is happening. This is kind of new to me. I'm a little scared. [*Here is an example of what often happens in this work. If the therapist makes a mistake, as long as they acknowledge it, clients are usually very generous in their responses.*]

Therapist: Is your being scared mean I should back off for a while from my focus on inner communication, or is it the kind of fear that can be expected when trying something new?

Emma: [*She smiles.*] I hate when you are right. I remember you telling me therapy would be hard sometimes. [*This is a positive development and has come about due to Emma's motivation to be engaged in therapy, as well as the therapist being willing to self-disclose, as described previously.*]

Therapist: If you want, I can push it a little harder and make a suggestion for something you can do between now and our next session.

Emma: Do I have a choice?

Therapist: Of course you do. And even if you let me make the suggestion, you still don't have to actually do it. [*This statement mitigates some of the risks of assigning homework. Clients often do not follow through with the homework, which can amplify their tendency toward self-criticism or even self-hatred.*]

Emma: Yeah. Lay it on me. But don't be surprised if I don't do it.

Therapist: Okay, here goes. Take a few minutes each day to check inside to see if any of the others would like to talk to you. Then, if it's okay with them, you could write down what they say in your journal. They might even have some ideas about how to resolve your conflict with your sister.

Emma: I'll think about it.

Therapist: Fair enough. I'll see you next week.

Emma: Okay. Bye.

At the next session, the therapist might ask how the week went and if Emma decided to try communicating with the others inside or not. If Emma decides to continue to discuss her conflict with her sister, the conversation, by necessity, will also include exploration of her inner system, given what was discussed in this session. On the other hand, if she brings a different problem to the session, the therapist will find ways to bring in the three pillars. This relieves the therapist from any pressure to somehow resolve the sister conflict for Emma, and it recognizes Emma's agency to find a resolution through her inner resources. At the same time, the therapeutic goals, as represented by the three pillars, take prominence in the work.

CHAPTER 10

THE INNER WORLD

As described in chapter 5, it can be helpful to think of a client's inner world as a paracosm, and your first task is to suspend disbelief about this inner realm being real, as it is in fact more real than the outside world to the alters inside. Aspiration 6 becomes relevant in this regard: "Have the courage to enter the client's inner realm while always staying grounded in this realm."

It can, however, be a challenge to figure out how to do this. Obviously, you cannot actually enter your client's inner world because it only exists inside their brain. This is where the first form of resourcing—attunement—plays a prominent role. If you hope to grasp some small sense of your client's inner world, you must first have the capacity to access your own. Siegel (2011) calls this *mindsight* and defines it as "a kind of focused attention that allows us to see the internal workings of our own minds" (p. ix). You must then exhibit empathy, which Siegel defines as "the capacity to create mindsight images of other people's minds" (p. 28). As discussed in chapter 1, there is no doubt that our brains have the capacity to create rich models of our own mind as well as models of others in our lives (Bennett, 2023).

Express your curiosity by asking questions—in line with aspiration 4: "Foster an abundance of curiosity regarding your client's system." Your client will hopefully share details about how they experience their inner world. Here is an example dialogue as to how such a conversation might go:

Blake: [*Blake is the primary.*] Natalie keeps trying to talk to me—that's why I can't seem to focus today.

Therapist: Please remind me who Natalie is.

Blake: She's a teenager, and she's very annoying—always criticizing me.

Therapist: Would it be okay if we paused what we had been talking about and turn our attention to Natalie?

Blake: I'd rather not, but I suppose it might be best. Otherwise, she will keep interrupting my stream of thought.

Therapist: Could you close your eyes and check in with her, perhaps finding out what her concerns are?

Blake: She is far away but yelling at me through a kind of tunnel.

Therapist: I'd like to be able to visualize this. Can you describe the tunnel?

Blake: [*He closes his eyes.*] It's a tube-like structure with an opening right near me, but it extends down to another level.

Therapist: If you look through the opening, can you see Natalie?

Blake: [*He opens his eyes.*] I've never tried to do that. Hold on. [*He closes his eyes again.*] No. I can't see very far because the tunnel turns, but I can hear her, plain as day.

Therapist: What is she saying?

Blake: [*He opens his eyes.*] She says, "Don't be such a wimp."

Therapist: Can she hear me talking?

Blake: Yeah.

Therapist: [*The therapist visualizes an image of the tunnel.*] I am trying to imagine what the tunnel looks like. How large is the opening that is near you?

Blake: Big enough for one person to walk through, but it would be a little tight.

Therapist: Have you ever walked into it?

Blake: No, I'm not sure I'd want to.

Therapist: Has Natalie ever walked though it close enough so you could see her?

Blake: Not that I remember. Oh, wait, I can hear her making thumping noises. I think she is getting closer. [*He closes his eyes.*] She's nearby. Oh! I see her now.

Therapist: Can you describe her?

Blake: Tall, wearing jeans with holes in them and a halter top. Long brown hair, lots of piercings. She wants to talk to you. [*He shifts slightly in the chair.*]

Natalie: [*She opens her eyes.*] Blake is useless.

Therapist: Hi Natalie. It's so good to meet you.

Natalie: Same here. I've been waiting for an invitation. I'm glad you are seeing Blake. He needs a lot of help, and I'm at my wit's end.

Therapist: He told me you often criticize him.

Natalie: Somebody has to get him to man up a little. He's such a wimp—lets people walk all over him.

Therapist: I see. So, your criticisms are designed to help him get stronger with his friends?

Natalie: His friends, his coworkers, his family.

Therapist: Is he nearby? Can he hear us talking?

Natalie: [*She closes her eyes, then opens them.*] I can't see him right now.

Therapist: Is the tunnel still there?

Natalie: Yeah, but he isn't in the tunnel. I don't know where he went.

Therapist: Please help me visualize what things look like inside.

Natalie: There is the tunnel. It runs straight ahead then turns to the right, and then it goes down another level.

Therapist: Can you describe what is outside the tunnel?

Natalie: Nothing important—a bunch of rooms. I've never explored this level.

Therapist: What level do you spend most of your time in?

Natalie: My home is one level below this level. I have a cabin by the beach.

Therapist: And Blake?

Natalie: What about Blake?

Therapist: I was just wondering where he goes when he isn't occupying the body.

Natalie: You'd have to ask him. Listen, I don't really like being out here. Blake's body is a little too crude for me. I need to go. I only came out to ask you if you could be a little tougher on him so that I could let up a little.

Therapist: I appreciate your feedback. I'll talk it over with Blake. Thanks for coming out to meet me.

Natalie: No problem. Bye. [*She closes her eyes.*]

Blake: [*He opens his eyes and looks around.*] What happened?

Therapist: Blake?

Blake: Yeah, it's me.

Therapist: I've been talking to Natalie. Could you hear us?

Blake: Not really.

Therapist: She told me about the tunnel and her cabin by the beach one level below you.

Blake: Really?

Therapist: Yes, I'll fill you in on what we discussed, but before you forget, can you remember where you went?

Blake: I'm not sure. [*He closes his eyes, then opens them.*] Wait a minute. I was inside a closet.

Therapist: Can you remember where the closet is and how you got there?

Blake: No, it's really fuzzy.

Therapist: Did you walk down the tunnel?

Blake: No, I did walk though. I remember that. There was a big house. I think I went in the front door and crawled into a closet.

Therapist: Was there anyone else around?

Blake: It's all fading away. I don't remember. I'm sorry doc. I can't remember. [*He starts to tear up.*] Maybe Natalie's right. I am a wimp.

At this point, the therapist decides to ignore Blake's self-deprecating remark in order to focus on the positive development of Blake's growing awareness of the internal world. The therapist also reasons that in order to be helpful to the whole system, such a discussion would involve the conflictual relationship between Blake and Natalie, and perhaps other alters who might have a more positive view of Blake. There is ample time in the future for such a conversation.

Therapist: I'm glad you are able to remember a little bit. This seems quite new to you.

Blake: [*He begins to regain his composure.*] Yeah, my head hurts.

Therapist: There's no hurry. I learned some things about your inner world. I tried to visualize it in my own mind. Are you curious about it?

Blake: I never thought about it much. A little bit curious, I guess. It seems pretty scary though. I'm not used to thinking about the inside.

At this point, there many ways the conversion can go. Regardless, the therapist will need to share with Blake a little about Natalie's concerns. Several sessions could easily be devoted to this new insight—that is, that Natalie wants Blake to become stronger. The therapist might assist Blake in learning some problem-solving skills or help him set some boundaries in his relationships. Perhaps, at some point, the therapist can encourage Natalie to intervene in a different way—for example, by encouraging Blake to practice some of his new skills rather than criticizing him when he doesn't do so.

Throughout this therapeutic work with Blake, the therapist can continue to be curious about the inner world and learn more about the tunnel, Natalie's beach cabin, Blake's big house with the closet, and whether there are other alters inhabiting the house, the beach, or any additional levels that the tunnel traverses.*

The outer and inner worlds influence and reflect each other in many ways. As a result, any shifts in the inner world will have real-life effects in the outside world. Sometimes those effects will be immediately experienced as positive. Other times, changes in the inner world that are clearly perceived as positive both by the client and therapist will result in negative consequences in the outside world. For example, when clients first experiment with conscious communication among alters, there will be some gradual dissolution of dissociative barriers. In the case of Blake and Natalie, as they become more curious about the big house, the tunnel, and the other levels, other alters who have been rather dormant may emerge and wish for some recognition. Some may discover the tunnel and have easier access to fronting the body. Not clear as to the rules and regulations in the outside world, these alters might create some drama or chaos. One way to help circumvent this is to conduct regular internal system meetings.

REGULAR INTERNAL SYSTEM MEETINGS

Regular internal system meetings are a way for the client to navigate disagreements among the alters; set some ground rules as to when it is okay for switching to occur; give all alters a forum to express their hopes, dreams, and concerns; and make decisions as to the best care for alters who are in pain. It is also a powerful way for you to encourage the client to be curious about their system while you embrace aspiration 4 for yourself: "Foster an abundance of curiosity regarding the client's system." These meetings are also an excellent way to continue working on the third pillar (the three Cs) in between sessions.

These meetings work best if the system has already established one or more responsible adults who have agreed to make the final decisions regarding actions to take in the outside world. It will be up to the client to decide how often to hold these meetings, but a rule of

* The tunnel, the big house, and the beach cabin are structures present in this particular imaginary client system. Please do not expect to find tunnels, big houses, or beach cabins when exploring inner worlds with your clients. There are no templates for how inner worlds will be organized, including what habitable or uninhabited spaces you and your clients might find there.

thumb is they should occur at least once a week. Some clients find it helpful to have them daily. If clients need help in starting these meetings, you can assist with the first one or two meetings, with the hope that the client will then take over on their own.

One way to structure an internal meeting is for the client to create ground rules. It is completely up to the client to set these rules, but here are some suggestions:

1. One alter agrees to take notes. That alter will, of course, need to be fronting the body at the time of the meeting. They can write in a journal or choose a different method, such as keeping notes in their phone.
2. All alters are invited to attend the meeting, but they are not required to attend.
3. Every alter has a right to present their views.
4. Every alter has the right to call a special meeting if needed.
5. Cooperation and compromises will be sought when discussing conflicting concerns or ideas.
6. If consensus cannot be reached, the responsible adult or adults will make any necessary final decisions, with the understanding that further discussion will be welcomed in future meetings.

Even if your client is successful in setting up reasonable ground rules, it may take some time for all the alters to follow them. Just as all of us have likely faced some difficulties in staff meetings in our work, these complications are likely to appear in internal system meetings as well. Some alters might refuse to attend the meetings. Others may dominate the discussion. Emotions may escalate. The responsible adults running the meetings might get fed up. You can assist your client when these difficulties arise by explaining that it may take some time for these conflicts to be ironed out and encouraging them to persist in the meantime.

When positive outcomes occur as a result of internal system meetings, the alters will hopefully strengthen their commitment toward ongoing communication and cooperation. For example, let's say a new trauma occurs in the client's life: a loved one dies or a partner assaults them. Rather than initiating a series of rapid switches with significant amnesia and real-world negative consequences, the client calls an emergency internal system meeting. In that meeting, intense emotional reactions of several alters are soothed, and the client sets up an emergency therapy session to make further plans to deal with the crisis. Although the therapist contributed to helping the client resolve the crisis, the internal system meeting is also acknowledged as a powerful method of dealing with such emergent issues.

INFORMED CONSENT

Informed consent is obviously important in working with any clients, as you must ensure the necessary consent forms are signed and understood at the beginning of therapy. With clients with DID, informed consent takes on a new meaning. Since you are working with a client with many different identities, it will frequently happen that one or more alters will not agree with the direction therapy is going, or they may object to the fact that the client is participating in therapy at all. Indeed, it is naive to think that every alter will be in agreement with therapy in general, or with specific inquiries that occur in the process. As you are able to identify and acknowledge alters, you must be willing to listen to each of their concerns.

Protective alters, in particular, may not be on board with therapy for a number of reasons. They may not trust you due to their previous experiences with health care professionals. They may worry that the primary will share a secret that could put an alter or the system as a whole in harm's way—for example, the abuser could follow up with a previous threat of violence were this secret to be revealed. Protectors may also worry that the primary might get stronger during therapy and, as a result, it will lessen their ability to influence the primary. Until you address these concerns, the protector might act in ways that sabotage therapy. For example, they might deceive the primary to ensure they don't show up for appointments or send threatening texts or voicemails to the therapist.

One way of conceptualizing this process is to realize that the protector alter has not given informed consent. The task then becomes to educate the alter sufficiently to obtain such consent, or absent that, a commitment to stand aside and not disrupt therapy. On a positive note, once the offending protector is acknowledged for their role in trying to protect the primary alter, it is often possible to reeducate the protector as to how they can protect the primary in more effective ways. Protectors often become the strongest allies in the therapeutic process.

Above all, the use of informed consent will reemerge frequently when working with clients with DID, and it must be dealt with in an open and nonjudgmental way. Here are some general suggestions to guide this process:

1. When a client is first diagnosed with DID, it is a good time to ask if all the alters agree with continuing therapy. If one or more object, explore the purpose and goals of therapy, and gather input as to the concerns the alter or alters have.

2. Even if a working agreement is reached, alters, especially protectors, may bring up other issues as therapy progresses. With any issue, psychoeducation, negotiation,

and clarification can all be helpful in reaching a compromise where the alter's concerns are acknowledged and a plan is put in place to ensure that their needs are respected.

3. If a client who rarely misses an appointment begins cancelling or no-showing, this is an opportunity to reopen the question whether there are one or more alters who are upset with you or who no longer wish to continue with therapy.
4. When the client is ready to engage in a more structured bottom-up therapy process (see chapter 11), informed consent becomes paramount. All known alters must either specifically agree to do the work or agree to stand back and allow the work to continue. Otherwise, there is a danger that they will interrupt the processing or that dissociative barriers will be broken down too quickly, leading to decompensation.

In all these cases, and many others that will come about, it is important to remember to never take sides in a disagreement between alters, and instead embrace the following aspirations: "Remind yourself that your client is the whole system, not any particular alter" (aspiration 2), and "Center the client system in therapy rather than centering yourself as the expert" (aspiration 3).

JOURNALING

Journaling is a wonderful intervention that allows clients to reflect on their personal experiences; keep track of their thoughts, feelings, hopes, goals, and dreams; and develop greater insight and self-awareness. Many of you are already using journaling in your practice with a wide range of clients, and the following safety issues will be relevant for all clients, including those with DID. Prior to encouraging a client to begin to keep a journal, you want to make sure they can keep it confidential and free from the eyes of others with whom they do not wish to share their innermost thoughts and feelings. If not, the benefits of journal writing can be outweighed by the negative consequences of having a client's secrets revealed without their consent.

If the client is not sure whether their journal would remain safe, you can help them take certain precautions. For example, they can keep their journal in a place where no one else would find it. If they own their own car, they can keep it in the trunk. Some clients prefer to use their phones, which are password-protected, to keep their journals in either a written, auditory, or visual manner. Once it is determined that the journal will be safe, it is important to let the client know that they are free to share portions of the journal with you, but this is never required. An additional consideration when working with clients with DID is to get input from all known alters. I have worked with clients with DID who have had their journal hidden or destroyed due to one or more alters objecting to what was written. It is best to work out these objections prior to the client starting the journal.

Once you get agreement among alters, the client's journal can be a handy place to facilitate ongoing communication among the alters, as well as a convenient place to record notes taken during internal system meetings. I often suggest that clients sit down with their journal and let all the alters know that, if they wish, they can take over the body and record their thoughts, ideas, and concerns. Then the responsible adult or adults will read, listen, or watch the entries and respond to journal entries at a later time. This provides alters who are too shy to talk directly to the primary or to the therapist an opportunity to share and be heard.

For example, let's say a client has a female child alter who is very shy and is unwilling to front the body to meet you. In addition, this child alter is frightened of the primary and hides under their bed (in the internal world) whenever you suggest the primary attempt to communicate with her. This child alter hears about the journal and pops out for a few minutes to draw a picture of a little baby and a big man. When the client shows you the picture in session, an adolescent alter who was selected to watch over the child pops out and tells you that she tried to stop the child alter from drawing the picture. From there, you can help the client educate the adolescent as to the importance of allowing ways for the child alter to continue to communicate, eventually discovering what the picture depicts.

Journaling is an important tool to facilitate inner communication. Although clients' systems generally require some hierarchical structures—that is, responsible adults need to make final decisions regarding important real-world actions—journaling provides a more egalitarian method to empower all alters to have a say in how the system operates.

CHAPTER 11

TRAUMA PROCESSING CONSIDERATIONS

Even though having some reliable information about how much abuse and neglect your client experienced in childhood could be helpful in your therapeutic work, I do not recommend that you ask questions seeking that information. The one exception to this is some gentle inquiries you must make during the assessment process. Once you have enough data to confirm an OSDD or DID diagnosis, there is no need to inquire further. (Note how aspiration 3 applies here: "Center the client system in therapy rather than yourself as the expert.")

There are three reasons for this. First, it is not necessary to know the details of the childhood trauma your client experienced in order to embrace the ten aspirations and engage the client using the three pillars. Second, as therapy progresses, the client will very likely begin to volunteer some of that information. When this happens, it is often more helpful to slow down the process rather than pursuing more information with further questions, as slowing down reduces risk of retraumatization, rapid switching, and decompensation. Third, as explored in chapter 7, the details of traumatic memories must be considered unreliable.

Nevertheless, as the client system becomes stabilized internally and their life in the outside world becomes less chaotic, there will likely be situations where the client becomes overwhelmed by traumatic memories, and it is important for you to know how to be most helpful when this occurs. One useful way to understand therapeutic approaches in working with clients with DID is to distinguish between top-down and bottom-up therapy. In short, top-down therapy helps clients rearrange and reframe problematic thoughts and feelings, while bottom-up therapy involves going deeper into the unconscious to reprocess traumatic memories (Corrigan & Hull, 2018; Kezelman & Stavropoulos, 2012; Nooney, 2022; van der Kolk, 2014).

In considering the differences between top-down versus bottom-up therapy, certain interventions can be clearly defined. For example, CBT is a good example of top-down therapy, while EMDR is a good example of bottom-up therapy. However, there are numerous interventions and therapeutic strategies that fall in between these two modalities that are more difficult to categorize. The best practices described in this book fall into this intermediary category. Sometimes, they are closer to the top-down definition, such as doing problem-solving with a particular alter. Other times, they clearly fall in the bottom-up category, like facilitating a healing conversation between a primary alter and a hidden-away child alter who is stuck reexperiencing a traumatic memory. There are occasions, however, when a specific bottom-up therapeutic modality, such as EMDR or CRM,* can be helpful in working through a specific traumatic event. In reflecting on these choices, be sure to remember aspiration 1: "Remember that your client has crucial 'insider knowledge,' whereas you only possess 'outsider knowledge.'"

Prior to implementing one of these interventions, it is essential that you have a strong attunement between yourself and the client. It is also important that you have a good understanding of parts work and dissociation, including the risk of dissociative barriers becoming loosened too quickly, as discussed in chapter 6. You want to pay attention to the stability of the system, both internally and externally, and ensure that you have informed consent from the parts before proceeding. And as with all therapeutic endeavors, you must work in collaboration with the whole client system to determine if and when these bottom-up therapeutic modalities should be utilized.

SLOWING DOWN THE PROCESS

Once the therapist and client establish a trusting therapeutic relationship, it is not unusual for a client with DID to begin sharing traumatic memories. This creates a dilemma for the therapist. On the one hand, it provides crucial data about the extent of the person's past

* Top-down therapies focus on insight and cognitive behavioral interventions, while bottom-up therapies address the "physical, sensorimotor, and experiential process as well as cognitions and verbal expressions of emotion" (Kezelman & Stavropoulos, 2012, as described in Nooney, 2023, p. 139). The following are all bottom-up modalities, although this list is not exhaustive: EMDR, brainspotting, CRM, somatic archaeology, IFS, sensorimotor psychotherapy, somatic experiencing, and accelerated experiential dynamic processing.

trauma and information that may have been missing from the initial assessment due to the client's initial lack of trust. On the other hand, there is a real risk that the client might become emotionally flooded and experience retraumatization. This is because the sharing itself will likely result in a weakening of some of the dissociative barriers that were erected between alters. In addition, some alters may wish to quickly share these memories, as they can talk about them without emotion and in a matter-of-fact way. You can think of these alters as *reporters*. The problem is that other alters in the system may get bombarded with memories they have been working hard to keep at bay, creating emotional disruption to the system.

As a sensitive and welcoming therapist, you might be inclined to remain silent as the reporter describes their detailed memories of abuse. In fact, there will be times when this approach is the best one. There are other times, however, when it is preferable to interrupt the client and suggest that the reporter check inside to determine whether all are okay with continuing. Aspiration 2 becomes relevant here: "Remind yourself that your client is the whole system, not any particular alter." The reporter, by beginning to share details about past abuse, has by default given consent. It would be a mistake, however, to assume that all the other alters in the system have consented to sharing that particular content. As the reporter begins their account, they may be unaware that others in the system object, in which case a number of events may occur:

1. The client shuts down into a dissociative state. This could occur due to a protective alter stopping the process.
2. The client abruptly changes the subject as another alter takes over the body.
3. A protective alter takes over fronting the body and expresses anger at you.
4. The client precipitously leaves the office.
5. The client continues sharing with you, and you both assess the session as being productive. The client then no-shows or cancels their next session due to protective alters no longer trusting the process. During this time, the risk of self-harm or suicide can increase.

If any of these events occur, all is not lost, as there will still be opportunities for you to provide assistance to the client by following aspiration 4—"Foster an abundance of curiosity regarding the client's system"—to discover what has occurred and make it possible to move forward in therapy. However, it would be preferable to anticipate some of these events occurring and intervene immediately to slow the process down.

CREATING A TRAUMA LIST

One way to slow the process down is to interrupt the client, praise them for their willingness to share, and suggest that, rather than go into the details of the memory immediately, they document information about the event in a trauma list. For example, this can include some or all of the following: the client's age at the time, a list of which alters were involved, a very brief description of what happened, and the name of the perpetrator or perpetrators. You would then explain that you'll keep this trauma list in a confidential file, and when therapy progresses to a point where it would be helpful to process the memory, you can retrieve the list and the client can decide which memory to work on. You would also do well to ask the reporting alter to consult with others in the system as to their opinions regarding what to share and when to share it.

During this process, if the reporter is successful in consulting with other alters, or if a protective alter emerges, you could facilitate a crucial conversation with that protector. You could reiterate that the client is not required to share anything until they are ready and that you know effective ways, when the time is right, to assist the client in processing painful memories safely so that healing can occur. If you discover that a particular protector is concerned that the reporter might continue to share information that is supposed to be secret, you can attempt to form an alliance with that protector, working together to ensure the reporter doesn't share too much information too quickly.

This also opens the door for the protector to develop a trusting relationship with you at their own pace. It also gives you time, with the assistance of the reporter or other alters, to help the protector understand that although sharing was dangerous when the client was little, things are different now. The protector might not fully understand that the body is all grown up, and the risk of the abuse happening again has been diminished and is very likely no longer present.

BOTTOM-UP THERAPY INTERVENTIONS

When you and the client system are in agreement that a specific bottom-up therapeutic intervention would be safe to implement, I recommend that you take certain precautions and put a plan in place prior to simply following the protocols and fidelity of the model.

Remember that internal walls are built carefully and for a reason, so when you begin to process trauma, the following challenges may present themselves:

1. Protectors may intentionally sabotage the process.
2. The primary alter running the show may quickly decompensate.
3. Suicidal or self-harming alters may act out.
4. Child alters may be further traumatized.

In order to protect the client from these negative outcomes, decide ahead of time when the processing session will take place and make some initial decisions. This includes deciding which particular memory will be processed and determining which alter or alters were directly involved in that memory. After this is settled, you must consider the following steps:

1. Talk to each of those alters and decide on their preferred resourcing method.
2. Solicit an alter who will volunteer to stay with each alter who is processing the memory, and provide the kind of support that alter desires—this might be energetic support, spiritual support, or physical support, such as holding hands.
3. Solicit a volunteer who will agree to stay with each alter for support after the session is over and until the next session. It can be the same alter or a different one.
4. If child alters are not involved in the processing, a responsible alter must be designated to watch over the children in their safe internal space, where they can be sheltered from the intensity of the processing.
5. If one or more child alters is directly involved in the memory being processed, increase the amount of support offered to them.
6. Those alters who are not directly involved in the processing or the support need to decide whether they want to witness the processing or not.
7. Determine ahead of time which responsible adult will agree to be available at the end of the session to make sure the system gets home safely.

On the designated day of processing, go over the plan again and make any changes, if necessary. Remember to be flexible, postponing the processing if needed, and don't expect everything to go as planned. Once you begin the processing, use whichever modality you have chosen to help the client process the trauma memory. Since I am most familiar with

EMDR, BSP, and CRM, the following suggestions map more closely with those modalities. This might involve:

1. Assisting each alter who was involved in the traumatic experience to be resourced
2. Asking the client to recall the memory
3. Connecting the memory to bodily sensations
4. Naming the emotional reaction or feeling associated with the memory
5. Rating the intensity of these emotions using a SUD rating scale
6. Providing additional resourcing if needed
7. Checking in with the supporting alters to make sure they are able to continue to do their work
8. Assisting supporting alters in resourcing if needed
9. Processing the memory

The following dialogue illustrates how each of these points might look in practice:

Therapist: Okay, Anita, let's review our plan. As the primary, you'll be watching over our work today, but you won't be directly involved in the processing of the memory. Is that your understanding?

Anita: Yes.

Therapist: So first, let's review the decisions that the other alters have made regarding their involvement.

Anita: So, the main person who remembers the event is Arya. She's twelve. She will be supported by Ben during the session today. He's seventeen. The two of them are pretty close, but Ben has no memory of the event.

Therapist: Sounds good. Now, we decided last time that there was no other alter who experienced this traumatic event. Is this your understanding?

Anita: Well, I sort of remember it, but I think that is because Arya told me about it recently. It was shortly after our meeting last week.

Therapist: Oh, I see. It's possible that some of the difficult emotions connected to the memory might get transferred to you during the processing. Perhaps we should reconsider the role you will be playing in the work today.

Anita: What do you mean?

Therapist: Rather than staying close to monitor and organize, you could step away and go to your room, for instance.

Anita: No, I'll be fine.

Therapist: Okay, if you are sure. I think it would be important for you to get resourced along with Arya and Ben before we start the processing.

Anita: Sure.

Therapist: Okay, how about the others?

Anita: Well, the child alters, Deon and Devon, are already in their playroom with the door closed, and Idris is inside watching over them. Maurice and Monica, the other teenagers, want to stand back and watch from a distance because they might want to do a session sometime in the future. Reuben plans to stay far away. As you know, he doesn't really like the idea of focusing on the past, but he has agreed not to interfere.

Therapist: Okay, are we missing anyone else?

Anita: No.

Therapist: Okay, can you ask Arya to front the body, and for you and Ben to stay close by and listen?

Arya: [*She closes and opens her eyes.*] I'm here.

Therapist: Arya?

Arya: That's me.

Therapist: Good to see you. Before we start, do you have any questions?

Arya: Not really. Do you really think this will work?

Therapist: I really do, but we can stop at any time if you need to.

Arya: I just want to get it over with.

Therapist: Okay, the first thing is to do some resourcing. The last time we met you said you really liked the Earth breathing technique. Have you been practicing it on your own?

Arya: Yes. It helps me stay calm.

Therapist: Before we start, can you check in with Ben and Anita to see if they are still nearby and if they would like to do the breathing with you, or if they would prefer a different form of resourcing?

Arya: [*She closes her eyes for a moment.*] Yes, they are nearby, and yes, they want to breathe with me.

Therapist: [*The therapist leads the three of them in Earth breathing.*] Okay, Arya, are you ready to begin?

Arya: Yeah. [*At this point, depending on the modality, some form of bilateral sound, light, or touch can be initiated. If doing BSP or CRM, certain eye positions can be set up.*]

Therapist: Okay, is Ben still with you?

Arya: Yeah, he's holding my hand.

Therapist: I invite you to recall the memory of when you were assaulted by your uncle.

Arya: I can see him. He has a mean look on his face.

Therapist: I invite you to focus on your body for a moment. Where do you feel the most distress?

Arya: My chest. Oh no, he's coming closer.

Therapist: See if you can freeze the image for a moment so we can slow this down.

Arya: Okay, I'm trying.

Therapist: See if you can move farther away from the image. Perhaps you can stand on a balcony looking down at him, something like that.

Arya: Ben is helping me. I am now standing in the corner. My uncle can't see me or get to me.

Therapist: How intense is your distress right now on a scale of 0 to 10?

Arya: I'm at a 6.

Therapist: What emotion is tied to that 6?

Arya: Fear.

Therapist: And where do you feel it in your body now?

Arya: Still in my chest.

Therapist: Okay. I invite you to just stay with it and see what happens next.

At this point, you would continue processing and proceed with the session according to your chosen modality. The primary difference would be the addition of any needed resourcing and the importance of supporting any alters—in this case, Ben. For this example, you would also need to pay attention to what else is happening in the system as a whole.

Therapist: Arya, I encourage you to take a little break and do some breathing with me, and to invite Ben to do it as well. [*They successfully engage in some breathing exercises.*] Okay, just rest a minute while I check in with Anita.

Anita: [*She opens and closes her eyes.*] I'm here.

Therapist: Have you been okay while this processing has been going on?

Anita: Yes. Maurice and Monica watched for a little while, then left.

Therapist: Can you tell if they are alright?

Anita: They're fine.

Therapist: And how about Reuben?

Anita: Actually, he showed up for a brief moment, shrugged, and then hid away again.

Therapist: And the kiddos?

Anita: Hold on a minute. [*She closes her eyes.*] I just spoke with Idris through the closed door to the playroom. She says they are fine at the moment. They've been coloring. Idris was a little worried about Devon because he drew a man lying on the floor with lots of blood dripping from his head.

Therapist: Could you talk to Idris again and see how Devon is doing now?

Anita: He's okay. He's playing checkers with Deon now.

Therapist: Good. I will go back to Arya now.

Arya: [*She closes and opens eyes.*] I'm here.

Therapist: Is Ben still with you?

Arya: Yeah.

Therapist: What's been happening while I was talking to the others?

Arya: I remembered something new.

Therapist: What was it?

Arya: There was someone else there.

Therapist: Do you know who?

Arya: My aunt.

Therapist: Do you want to continue processing?

Arya: For a little bit. My aunt and uncle are talking now.

At this point, the processing continues, and the therapist remains silent, carefully watching the client. After a few minutes, the therapist notices the client shift in her seat.

Therapist: What's happening now?

Arya: My aunt and uncle argued, then my aunt left. She just walked away and my uncle turned to me.

Therapist: Is Ben still with you?

Arya: Yes. Ben and I moved back to the corner again. Now my uncle is looking around for me.

Therapist: Do you want to continue?

Arya: Ben and I stepped out to face my uncle.

Therapist: What is your number now?

Arya: Going up fast.

Therapist: Can you and Ben step back and watch what happens from a distance?

Arya: We will try.

The therapist notices that additional processing is going on and is silent again. It is not necessary for the therapist to know all the details of what is happening during the processing. After a few minutes, the therapist speaks again.

Therapist: What is happening now?

Arya: My uncle left the room.

Therapist: See if you can keep going, to remember what happened next.

Arya: I went to the bathroom and cried.

Therapist: If you can tolerate it, see if you can watch yourself in the bathroom crying.

Arya: [*She closes her eyes and sits in silence for a moment.*] Okay, it's done now. [*She opens her eyes.*]

Therapist: What number are you now?

Arya: I'm at a 3, but it's all in my throat right now.

Therapist: We are almost out of time. Would this be an okay place to stop?

Arya: Yes.

Therapist: Please gather Ben and Anita near you, and we will do some more breathing together.

Arya: Okay, we're all breathing together. Now Ben and Anita are hugging me.

Therapist: Stay with your connection as long as you need to.

Arya: [*She speaks after a few moments of silence.*] Okay, we're okay now.

Therapist: You've done some powerful work today, Arya. How do you feel now?

Arya: Exhausted.

Therapist: Remember, Anita said she would stay with you and support you once you leave here and until our next session. Can you check in with her to make sure she is still able to do this?

Arya: She says yes. Ben says he will help too.

Therapist: Okay, sounds good. Can you let Anita back?

Anita: [*She closes and then opens her eyes.*] I'm here.

Therapist: How are you doing?

Anita: I'm more tired than I thought I'd be.

Therapist: Do you remember what Idris said about Devon's picture?

Anita: Yeah.

Therapist: I know you're exhausted, but could you check in with Idris and make sure she will be able to watch over Devon this week in case some new memories have popped up for him?

Anita: [*She pauses.*] I just spoke to her. She's on it.

Therapist: Excellent. Are you able to drive home?

Anita: I'm not sure.

Therapist:	Would you like to rest a bit first, or is there someone else you'd trust to drive?
Anita:	Ben says if I sit with Arya, he will drive.
Therapist:	Has Ben driven the car before?
Anita:	Lots of times.
Therapist:	Oh, I didn't realize he has been driving.
Anita:	He's 17, and very cautious. He's probably a better driver than I am.
Therapist:	Okay. Anything else you want to say before you go?
Anita:	It was pretty intense.
Therapist:	Yes. You all did really well today. I would suggest that you rest as much as you can between now and our next meeting. If any other memories or emotions come up, see if you can write them down in your journal. Be sure to let Idris know this as well, in case something more comes up with Devon. We'll use our next meeting to talk more about what happened today and where to go from here.
Anita:	Okay.
Therapist:	Also, as we discussed last time, you are free to text me if something comes up and you want me to know right away. Just remember, I might not get the text right away or be able to answer immediately, and your safety plan is still in operation.
Anita:	Yep. See you next week.

Once you have finished processing the memory, make sure to provide additional resourcing and remind the client of their in-between-session support plan. You can give the client a choice to immediately discuss what has just occurred, or to leave without further discussion. Either way, cnsurc a rcsponsiblc adult is fronting the body and is willing and able to make sure the client gets home safely. At the next session, be prepared to follow up by discussing the effects the client has experienced since the processing session. You can find additional information regarding the implementation of bottom-up therapeutic modalities with DID in *Diagnosing and Treating Dissociative Identity* (Nooney, 2022) and in the guidelines described by the ISSTD (2011).

MANAGING UNFORESEEN DECOMPENSATION

Processing intense traumatic memories is risky, so despite all the precautions you take, there will be times that, despite your best efforts, the client will suffer some distressing effects. For example, alters who are suicidal or who promote harming the body may emerge. Structures that were carefully set up to prevent rapid switching may break down due to a restructuring of the inner world. As mentioned previously, one way to reduce these risks is by setting up a comprehensive safety plan. This can include offering the client additional access to you by text, phone, or email, as well as offering additional scheduled sessions. Part of the plan can include reminding the client how to contact other members of their support network, as well as getting commitments from internal alters who volunteer to intervene if needed. Aspiration 10 is also important to remember: "Remind yourself that prior to your client meeting you, they have very likely lived through and survived much worse experiences than they are having now."

CONCLUSION

When working with clients with DID, you must honor the client's entire system, let go of outcome expectations, trust the process, and be in it for the long haul. Although this book has described several therapeutic interventions that are helpful for clients with DID, this does not preclude you from using other interventions that can be helpful in the treatment of complex trauma. This includes yoga, collective movement, music, theater, and neurofeedback (van der Kolk, 2014).

When it comes to neurofeedback in particular, I have gathered anecdotal evidence regarding a specific form of neurofeedback, known as *passive infrared hemoencephalography* (pIR HEG),* that can result in increased co-consciousness and self-efficacy in working with clients with DID.** I like this intervention because it is one of the simpler forms of neurofeedback, yet it addresses an essential problem that plagues many clients with developmental trauma, including clients with DID: difficulty regulating intense emotions.

In HEG, the client watches a movie while wearing a heat-sensitive sensor on their forehead that is connected to a computer. The sensor is passive in that it doesn't send any pulses or electrical signals into the person. Instead, the sensor reacts to increases and decreases in cerebral blood flow as the client watches the movie. When the client's prefrontal cortex activates and blood flow increases in that region, the brain must expel the increased heat. Similarly, when the client's limbic system activates due to surprise, fear, pleasure, or some other response, blood flow decreases in the prefrontal cortex. When the client's brain activates due to the movie, the sensor halts the video, and a bar graph then pops up on the screen, instructing the client to make the bar graph go up by calmly focusing on it. When the client achieves a calm focus, the sensor again picks up heat from the prefrontal cortex, and the movie starts up again, rewarding the client. After many sessions of HEG training, the brain becomes more efficient in calming down the limbic system and develops increased flexibility in shifting back and forth between a state of calm and activation. The result of this increased flexibility is a reduction in anxiety caused by an oversensitive amygdala and an increased capacity for focused attention.

* pIR HEG was initially developed by Dr. Jeffrey A. Carmen as a treatment for migraine headaches. See www.stopmymigraine.com for more information.

** T. P. Guenther, personal communication, July 10, 2023

When introducing HEG or any other neurofeedback intervention to a client with DID, it is important to get informed consent from all known alters, inviting those who wish to take part in the procedure to step forward and those who are not interested to step back. You should agree to stop at any time whenever any alter wishes to do so and make sure there is enough time at the end of the session to discuss any effects, positive or negative, on the system. Sebern Fisher (2014) also provides detailed information about how to implement a wide range of neurofeedback in working with clients with severe dissociation, including DID.

Ultimately, working with clients with DID presents challenges as well as wonderful opportunities. Therapists can grow in powerful ways as they learn to identify and resolve countertransference issues. However, they are at risk of secondary traumatic stress and compassion fatigue as they guide clients toward healing early childhood trauma and attachment wounds. When this occurs, aspiration 9 becomes relevant: "Seek out consultation and your own personal therapy when needed, especially when experiencing countertransference." Even the most seasoned therapists need individual or professional peer support to ensure that they can remain committed to this work.

If we hope to avoid our own downfall as therapists, it is also critical to make time for self-care activities that recharge and rejuvenate us. Although many self-care practices can be done alone, such as meditation and exercise, these are not sufficient for self-care to be beneficial. Just as clients need a balance between doing inner work and making changes in their daily lives in the outside world, the same is true for therapists. Humans are social creatures, so there must be a community component to self-care. Therefore, in your personal life, make it a point to reach out to others and to continue to build and sustain meaningful relationships. This provides an antidote to compassion fatigue and burnout.

REFERENCES

Allshorn, G. (2021, April 5). *We are all Spock. Humanist Blog.* https://humanist-world.net/2021/04/05/we-are-all-spock

American Psychiatric Association. (1987). *Diagnostic and statistical manual of mental disorders* (3rd ed., rev.).

American Psychiatric Association. (2013). *Diagnostic and statistical manual of mental disorders* (5th ed.). https://doi.org/10.1176/appi.books.9780890425596

American Psychiatric Association. (2022). *Diagnostic and statistical manual of mental disorders* (5th ed., text rev.). https://doi.org/10.1176/appi.books.9780890425787

Anderson, F. G. (2021). *Transcending trauma: Healing complex PTSD with Internal Family Systems Therapy.* PESI Publishing, Inc.

Anderson, F. G., Sweezy, M., & Schwartz, R. C. (2017). *Internal Family Systems skills training manual: Trauma-informed treatment for anxiety, depression, PTSD & substance abuse.* PESI Publishing, Inc.

Anderson, F. G., & Sweezy, M. (2016). What IFS offers to the treatment of trauma. In M. Sweezy & E. L. Ziskind (Eds.), *Innovations and elaborations in Internal Family Systems Therapy* (pp. 133–147). Routledge.

Armstrong, J. G., Putnam, F. W., Carlson, E. B., Libero, D. Z., & Smith, S. R. (1997). Development and validation of a measure of adolescent dissociation: The Adolescent Dissociative Experiences Scale. *Journal of Nervous and Mental Disease, 185*(8), 491–497. https://doi.org/10.1097/00005053-199708000-00003

Bennett, M. (2023). *A brief history of intelligence: Evolution, AI, and the five breakthroughs that made our brains. Mariner Books.*

Brand, B. L., Sar, V., Stavropoulos, P., Krüger, C., Korzekwa, M., Martínez-Taboas, A., & Middleton, W. (2016). Separating fact from fiction: An empirical examination of six myths about dissociative identity disorder. *Harvard Review of Psychiatry, 24*(4), 257–270. https://doi.org/10.1097/HRP.0000000000000100

Brenner, G. H. (2023, September/October). Authenticity: Seeking realness in an increasingly artificial world. *Psychology Today*, 26–31.

Carlson, E. B., & Putnam, F. W. (1993). An update on the Dissociative Experience Scale. *Dissociation: Progress in the Dissociative Disorders, 6*(1), 16–27.

Conklin, C. Z., & Westen, D. (2005). Borderline personality disorder in clinical practice. *American Journal of Psychiatry, 162*(5), 867–875. https://doi.org/10.1176/appi.ajp.162.5.867

Corrigan, F. M., & Hull, A. M. (2018). The emerging psychological trauma paradigm: An overview of the challenge of current models of mental disorder and their treatment. *International Journal of Cognitive Analytic Therapy & Relational Mental Health, 2*, 121–146.

Fine, C. G. (1988). The work of Antoine Despine: The first scientific report on the diagnosis and treatment of a child with multiple personality disorder. *American Journal of Clinical Hypnosis, 31*, 33–39. https://doi.org/10.1080/00029157.1988.10402765

International Society for the Study of Trauma and Dissociation. (2011). Guidelines for treating dissociative identity disorder in adults, third revision. *Journal of Trauma & Dissociation, 12*(2), 115–187. https://doi.org/10.1080/15299732.2011.537247

Fisher, S. F. (2014). *Neurofeedback in the treatment of developmental trauma: Calming the fear-driven brain.* W. W. Norton.

Gibson, R. (2008). *My body, my Earth: The practice of somatic archaeology*. iUniverse.

Grand, D. (2013). *Brainspotting: The revolutionary new therapy for rapid and effective change*. Sounds True.

Kezelman, C., & Stavropoulos, P. (2012). *Practice guidelines for treatment of complex trauma and trauma informed care and service delivery*. Blue Knot Foundation.

Khoury, M. J., & Valdez, R. (2016, February 17). Rare diseases, genomics and public health: An expanding intersection. *Centers for Disease Control and Prevention.* https://blogs.cdc.gov/genomics/2016/02/17/rare-diseases

Kluft, R. P. (2009). A clinician's understanding of dissociation: Fragments of an acquaintance. In P. F. Dell & J. A. O'Neil (Eds.), *Dissociation and the dissociative disorders: DSM-V and beyond* (pp. 599–623). Routledge.

Loewenstein, R. J. (1991). An office mental status examination for complex chronic dissociative symptoms and multiple personality disorder. *Psychiatric Clinics, 14*(3), 567–604. https://doi.org/10.1016/S0193-953X(18)30290-9

Loftus, E. F., & Pickrell, J. E. (1995). The formation of false memories. *Psychiatric Annals, 25*(12), 720–725. https://doi.org/10.3928/0048-5713-19951201-07

Marich, J. (2023). *Dissociation made simple: A stigma-free guide to embracing your dissociative mind and navigating daily life.* North Atlantic Books.

Maté, G. (2022). *The myth of normal: Trauma, illness & healing in a toxic culture*. Avery.

Montgomery, A. (2020, January 30). Interpersonal neurobiology and attachment. *Encyclopedia of Social Work*. NASW Press and Oxford University Press. https://doi.org/10.1093/acrefore/9780199975839.013.993

Morgan, A. (2000). *What is narrative therapy? An easy-to-read introduction*. Dulwich Centre Publications.

Nooney, G. L. (2022). *Diagnosing and treating dissociative identity disorder: A guide for social workers and all frontline staff.* NASW Press.

Nooney, G. L. (2023, August 23). Dissociative identity disorder. *Encyclopedia of Social Work*. NASW Press and Oxford University Press. https://oxfordre.com/socialwork/view/10.1093/acrefore/9780199975839.001.0001/acrefore-9780199975839-e-1633

O'Keane, V. (2021). *A sense of self: Memory, the brain, and who we are*. W. W. Norton.

Pulliam-Moore, C. (2022, April 27). How Moon Knight plays into Hollywood's obsession with dissociative identity disorder. *The Verge*. https://www.theverge.com/2022/4/27/23031165/moon-knight-dissociative-identity-disorder-marvel-disney-plus

Ranganath, C. (2024). *Why we remember: Unlocking memory's power to hold on to what matters*. Doubleday.

Ross, C. A. (1999). Subpersonalities and multiple personalities: A dissociative continuum? In J. Rowan & M. Cooper (Eds.) *The plural self: Multiplicity in everyday life* (pp. 183–197). Sage.

Ross, C. A. (2000). *The trauma model: A solution to the problem of comorbidity in psychiatry*. Manitou Communications, Inc.

Ross, C., & Halpern, N. (2009). *Trauma model therapy: A treatment approach for trauma, dissociation and complex comorbidity*. Manitou Communications.

Sar, V., Kundakci, T., Kiziltan, E., Yargic, I. L., Tutkun, H., Bakim, B., Bozkurt, O., Özpulat, T., Keser, V., & Özdemir, Ö. (2003). The Axis-I dissociative disorder comorbidity of borderline personality disorder among psychiatric outpatients. *Journal of Trauma & Dissociation, 4*(1), 119–136. https://doi.org/10.1300/J229v04n01_08

Schwartz, A. (2021). *The complex PTSD treatment manual: An integrative, mind-body approach to trauma recovery.* PESI Publishing, Inc.

Schwarz, L., Corrigan, F., Hull, A., & Raju, R. (2017). *The comprehensive resource model: Effective therapeutic techniques for the healing of complex trauma*. Routledge.

Shapiro, F., & Forrest, M. S. (2016). *EMDR: The breakthrough therapy for overcoming anxiety, stress, and trauma*. Basic Books.

Shorkey, C. T., & Uebel, M. (2013, September 3). Gestalt therapy. *Encyclopedia of Social Work*. NASW Press and Oxford University Press. https://oxfordre.com/socialwork/view/10.1093/acrefore/9780199975839.001.0001/acrefore-9780199975839-e-163

Siegel, D. J. (2011). *Mindsight: The new science of personal transformation*. Bantam Books.

Steinberg, M., & Schnall, M. (2001). *The stranger in the mirror: Dissociation—the hidden epidemic*. Cliff Street Books.

Stone, H., & Stone, S. L. (1989). *Embracing ourselves: The voice dialogue manual*. New World Library.

Taylor, M., Mottweiler, C. M., Naylor, E. R., & Levernier, J. G. (2015). Imaginary worlds in middle childhood: A qualitative study of two pairs of coordinated paracosms. *Creative Research Journal, 27*(2), 166–174. https://doi.org/10.1080/10400419.2015.1030318

Taylor, M., Mottweiler, C. M., Aguiar, N. R., Naylor, E. R., & Levernier, J. G. (2020). Paracosms: The imaginary worlds of middle childhood. *Society for Research in Child Development, 91*(1), 164–178. https://doi.org/10.1111/cdev.13162

Valdez, R., Ouyang, L., & Bolen, J. (2016, January 14). Public health and rare diseases: Oxymoron no more. *Centers for Disease Control and Prevention, 13*. http://dx.doi.org/10.5888/pcd13.150491

van der Kolk, B. A. (1994). The body keeps the score: Memory and the evolving psychobiology of posttraumatic stress. *Harvard Review of Psychiatry, 1*(5), 253–265. http://dx.doi.org/10.3109|/10673229409017088

van der Kolk, B. A. (2014). *The body keeps the score: Brain, mind, and body in the healing of trauma.* Penguin Books.

van der Kolk, B. A., Lanius, R., Ogden, P., Bryant, T., Levine, P., Fisher, J., Steele, K., & Brand, B. (2023). How to identify and treat dissociation (even when it is subtle) [Transcript of online conference presentation]. *National Institute for the Clinical Application of Behavioral Medicine.*

van der Kolk, B. A., McFarlane, A. C., & van der Hart, O. (1996). A general approach to treatment of posttraumatic stress disorder. In B. A. van der Kolk, A. C. McFarlane, & L. Weisaeth (Eds.), *Traumatic stress: The effects of overwhelming experience on mind, body, and society* (pp. 417–440). Guilford Press.

van Ijzendoorn, M. H., Schuengel, C., & Bakermans-Kranenburg, M. J. (1999). Disorganized attachment in early childhood: Meta-analysis of precursors, concomitants, and sequelae. *Development and Psychopathology, 11*(2), 225–249. https://doi.org/10.1017/S0954579499002035

White, M. (2007). *Maps of narrative practice.* W. W. Norton.

Williams, M., & Penman, D. (2011). *Mindfulness: An eight-week plan for finding peace in a frantic world.* Rodale.

Wilson, C., Pence, D. M., & Conradi, L. (2013, November 4). Trauma-informed care. *Encyclopedia of Social Work.* https://doi.org/10.1093/acrefore/9780199975839.013.1063

Wolpe, J. (1969). *Subjective Units of Distress Scale (SUDS)* [Database record]. APA PsycTests. https://doi.org/10.1037/t05183-000

ACKNOWLEDGMENTS

I would first like to acknowledge that my privileges as a straight, white, able-bodied, middle-class, married, cisgender male have helped open doors for me as my career developed, finally leading to the publication of this book. I have benefited from one other privilege that is less often mentioned but is especially helpful in doing this work, and like all other privileges, it was not earned by me but occurred due to the love and nurturing of my parents: growing up with a secure attachment status.

As I traveled along on my career journey, I was strongly influenced by key persons and events. The first seminal event was the Vietnam War. I was drafted, granted conscientious objector status, and ordered to perform alternate service at Threshold's, a rehabilitation clubhouse in Chicago for clients diagnosed with serious mental illness. I learned much from both the staff and members. My next stop was Loyola University, where many enthusiastic professors helped me experience the wonders and excitement of scholarship as I earned my MSW. I then spent seven years working in a state psychiatric hospital in North Carolina, where my understanding of mental illness was greatly enhanced by the patients who shared their lived experience with me.

My next career opportunity was an outpatient community mental health center in 1990. One of my first clients was a young woman with DID. I am thankful that my supervisor at the time, Lucille Swalve, sent me off to Minnesota for specialized training in DID, as no one at the mental health center at that time had any expertise in working with clients with dissociation.

Studying narrative therapy in Australia in 1999 with the late Michael White provided me with an underlying worldview and a set of therapeutic maps that:

1. Honored the lived experience and insider knowledge of the clients I worked with
2. Continued to influence me as I studied and applied various top-down and bottom-up therapeutic modalities over several decades of outpatient therapy work with clients with early childhood trauma, including those with a diagnosis of DID
3. Provided me with an antidote to burnout
4. Served as the substrate of the ten aspirations outlined in this book

I first approached PESI to do a workshop on DID in 2018. I am grateful to Ryan Bartholomew for taking a risk with me even though he was uncertain whether there would be enough interest in DID trainings to make the adventure financially feasible. Multiple in-person workshops evolved into webinars during the COVID-19 pandemic, and I was excited when Ryan referred me to PESI's publishing arm to consider writing a book. I had already published my first book in treating DID through NASW Press, and shortly thereafter an article in the *Encyclopedia of Social Work*. This new PESI book was envisioned to be a user-friendly guidebook. Kate Sample's enthusiasm inspired me to undertake the project, and Jenessa Jackson and Alissa Schneider's high quality editing and clarity of thought and expression has allowed for this book to be readable and, hopefully, useful for the busy therapists who are courageous enough to work with this population.

Lastly, I wish to acknowledge my wife and life partner of forty-four years, Ibu, who tolerated my many hours writing, isolated in my basement office.

ABOUT THE AUTHOR

Gregory L. Nooney, MSW, ACSW, LISW, LCSW, earned a master's degree in social work from Loyola University in Chicago in 1983 and is licensed in Iowa (LISW) and Hawaii (LCSW). He is the author of *Diagnosing and Treating Dissociative Identity Disorder: A Guide for Social Workers and All Frontline Staff*, published in 2022 by NASW Press, and an article entitled "Dissociative Identity Disorder" in the *Encyclopedia of Social Work*. Greg has worked as a therapist, mostly in community mental health centers, for forty years, and was the director of a mental health clinic from 2007 to 2017. Now semi-retired, he sees a few clients, does supervision, and offers consultation for other therapists who are working with clients with DID. Greg is currently in the process of writing a novel with a main character who has DID. He and his wife have four adult children and live in Iowa in a small house with two cats and a vegetable garden. Greg is passionate in his desire to educate other therapists to accept and work cooperatively with those who are diagnosed with OSDD or DID. He can be reached through his website at www.gregnooney.com.